The Change⁸

Insights into Self-Empowerment

Jim Britt ~ Jim Lutes

With

Co-authors From Around the World

The Change[8]

Jim Britt ~ Jim Lutes

All Rights Reserved

Copyright 2015

The Change

10556 Combie Road, Suite 6205

Auburn, CA 95602

The use of any part of this publication, whether reproduced, stored in any retrieval system or transmitted in any forms or by any means, electronic or otherwise, without the prior written consent of the publisher, is an infringement of copyright law.

Jim Lutes ~ Jim Britt

The Change[8]

SKU: 2370000285782

Co-authors

Mahri Best

Stephanie Chung

Tom Erik Green

Kevin Audley

Anne K. Uemura, PhD

Sharón Lynn Wyeth

Diana Allen

Sally K. O'Brien

Jorge Luis Aquino

Valerie Bernard

Johnny Morney

Jill Kovacovich

Mache Torres

Stephen Simpson

Mary Cheyne

Adrienne Slaughter

Mike Greenly

Marcus Cox

Nancy Proffitt

Nancy Bauser

The Change is proud to support

Good Women International

Every five minutes, one American child (many as young as ten years old) will be abducted and trafficked into the sex trade. 274 children a day. 100,000 each year and that estimate could be low. The total current number of human trafficking victims in the U.S. alone reaches into the hundreds of thousands, and worldwide into the millions.

All profits from the sale of Amazon Kindle electronic books are being donated to Good Women International, whose focus is on the prevention of sexual exploitation of young women and children. They support self-empowerment and educational programs worldwide designed to educate our youth to avoid becoming a victim. A recent successful project was an anti-trafficking curricula for our high schools which is now complete.

Enslavement is a reality. It is documented and it is real. The question is: What are we going to do about it?

To make a donation to Good Women International, a non-profit subsidiary of Village Care International, go to: www.SupportGoodWomen.com All donations are tax deductible under Tax ID #: 88-0471768. We welcome and appreciate your donations no matter how small.

GoodWomenInternational.org

Note: *Donations are never for salaries, as Good Women is a volunteer organization*

DEDICATION

This book is dedicated to all those seeking change

Foreword

Berny Dohrmann, Chairman of CEO Space International

To The Readers of *The Change* Series:

Jim Britt has been a mentor to *Chicken Soup* authors, and to some of the foremost thought leaders on earth. Jim Britt's groundbreaking work in *Letting Go*, releasing past traumas and betrayals in life to return once again to forward-looking manifestation within your full powers, has been instructing at leading *Fortune* companies and to standing-room-only seminars all over the world. For three decades, Jim Britt has been the "trainer of the trainers," of which I am only one. Jim has been an instructor at CEO Space, the most prestigious, hard to get into faculty on the planet, where he developed millions of dollars of resources as he assisted others to develop tens of millions of dollars for their own dream making. Jim is the most "unchanged by success and wealth" man I have ever known. He is an unselfish archangel, like in his book *Rings of Truth*.

Today, Jim Britt and Jim Lutes, along with many inspiring co-authors from around the world, bring a pioneering work to the market to transform your own journey into master manifestation. Their principles are forged on coaching millions on every continent. As you read, you are exploring self-development as the world has yet to practice. In fact, Jim and Jim's publications lead to this one APEX MOMENT. Everything you have done to date in your own life, everyone you have met, every lesson you have learned, has led you to this one GREAT life opportunity… the moment of your own transformation into ever-rising full potential.

As a five-time best-selling author myself, as a filmmaker, and with CEO Space, you can imagine how fussy I am to write a foreword to publications in the self-development space. CEO Space was just ranked by *Forbes Magazine* as the leading entrepreneur firm, which hosts five annual business growth conferences serving over 140 countries. It was also named by *Forbes* as THE MEETING in the world that YOU CANNOT AFFORD TO MISS. The world today demands more than a reputation defender to secure your forward brand; it requires that you take responsibility for your own brand and reputation in life. This book will inspire you to do just that.

CEO Space International has supported launches for many amazing works, including *Chicken Soup for the Soul; Men Are From Mars, Women Are From Venus; Rich Dad, Poor Dad; The Secret; No Matter What; Three Feet From Gold; Conversations With The King*; and now the movies *Growing Up Graceland* and *Wish Man* (for Make a Wish Foundation); *Outwitting the Devil* by Napoleon Hill and Sharon Lechter; Tony Robbins' great publications; of course Jim Britt's best-selling book *Rings of Truth;* and so many more. The totals have reached more than 2 billion eyeballs! You can't play around with that Mount Everest of credibility that I guard like a bank vault!

You can therefore appreciate why I encourage 100% of our followers of all the publications named to BUY JIM BRITT and JIM LUTES' book series *The Change* as a customer recognition for your own ten-best close relationships or clients. But don't just buy this book; rather, I endorse that you buy 10, and you giftwrap them to acknowledge your most important top ten relationships in life or clients in business. By doing so, you will retain more clients and encourage repeat buying. You may also receive more referrals and strengthen each relationship. The laws of giving will come back to you 10 to 1. When you give freely, you will always receive a rain into your life just as you rain into the lives of those you treasure. Jim

Britt, Jim Lutes, and the insightful and inspiring co-authors have given you in *The Change* series a great opportunity… more important than pouring ice water over someone's head on YouTube as a challenge for charity! The gift that keeps on giving begins when you step up and BUY 10, knowing you have been instrumental in inspiring 10 friends to live a better life. Together, we are going to reach 1 BILLION SOULS as we help Jim Britt, Jim Lutes, and their co-authors to achieve their goal to transform human consciousness in our lifetime. Like Zig Ziglar, Jim Rohn, the great Roger Anthony, and so many friends who have passed, my friend Jim Britt is now a historical event in every training, every publication, and every online work at CEO Space. If you ever have the opportunity, STOP YOUR LIFE and see JIM BRITT & JIM LUTES LIVE and you will thank me personally, I know.

Their work is powerful. You'll let go of the baggage you've been carrying around for years and learn to embrace everything that creates the future you want and deserve. As you close the pages of any of *The Change* books, you will say over and over again "THANK YOU Jim Britt and Jim Lutes for creating this work." You will gain a new life of super focus as never before and you will commence to master manifest in your own individual life as never before. *The Change* books provide tools to transform results for corporations, institutions, and individuals, and once applied it will be impossible to miss your future success in life.

In my opinion, there are only the following areas to embrace for each of us:

- Spiritual oneness and balance
- Recreational balance and nature
- Relationship where *Perfection Can Be Had!* (my book)
- Career attainment of goals that you, yourself, reset along the way

- Parenting either directly or by embracing a child you adopt to mentor at any and every age in life

These perspectives come into alignment within a framework of Jim Britt and Jim Lutes' imagination, along with decades of human-potential work. My advice is this work is a "BUY 10 TO SHARE WITH FRIENDS" pledge. In fact, a billion readers is a global path that Jim Britt and Jim Lutes are going to achieve NEXT for the world common good.

Let's help in this quest, as both men unselfishly donate their only asset, their precious LIFE TIME, to elevate one life at a time to their full potential and greatness.

My final request to all those who are reading my foreword is that you DO IT NOW. When you think of the good you will be doing, just ask yourself, "How long will I make them WAIT?"

I'm buying my 10 today!

Berny Dohrmann

Chairman, CEO Space International

P.S. I so approve this message for all my readers and followers worldwide. CEO Space has helped authors break the book of all records a half a dozen times, which means the only record to beat can be done with the publication you are buying 10 of now. Together, we are going to set a global record with one publication. Make the PLEDGE and give the gift of personal development. DO IT TODAY!

Table of Contents

Foreword ix

Jim Britt 1
    Commitment

Jim Lutes 13
    Universal Laws and Rules of the Mind

Valerie Bernard 27
    The Biggest Game-CHANGER

Johnny Morney 43
    Top 5 Global Networking Positions of Power Factors

Mike Greenly 57
    From "Stage Fright" to the Power of Authenticity

Mache Torres 69
    So Near Yet So Far

Mary Cheyne 81
    Conscious Communication: Your Prescription for Best Outcomes and Fulfilling Relationships

Stephen Simpson, MD 97
    Get Lucky Now! The Seven Secrets for Abundant Health, Wealth, and Happiness

Nancy Proffitt 111
    Managing Change by Changing Minds

Marcus Cox 123
    Going Beyond the Box

Tom Erik Green 135
    ThePlusCode ®: Change and the Image You Hold In Your Mind

Sharón Lynn Wyeth 147
    What Does Your Name Say About You?

Mahri Best 155
    Change is Choice

Diana Allen 167
    Be Your Own Healer

Stephanie Chung 181
    Mastering Change: Be Strong, Be Brave!

Nancy Bauser 191
    Accept, Survive, & Thrive

Anne K. Uemura, PhD 201
    Listen to the Cries of Your Heart

Jill Kovacovich, RN, BSN, PHN 215
    Damaged Goods to the Silver Lining (Unconditional Love)

Jorge Aquino 227
    The Decision

Sally K. O'Brien 237
    Love You More: My Last Month with Lael

Kevin Audley 247
    What If YOU Were Your Own Best Friend?

Adrienne Slaughter 261
    How an A-plus Attitude Turns Adversity into Achievement

Afterword 273

Jim Britt

Jim Britt is an internationally recognized leader in the field of peak performance and personal empowerment training. He is author of 13 best-selling books, including *Cracking the Rich Code; Cracking the Life Code; Rings of Truth; The Power of Letting Go; Freedom; Unleashing Your Authentic Power; Do This. Get Rich-For Entrepreneurs; The Flaw in The Law of Attraction;* and *The Law of Realization,* to name a few.

Jim has presented seminars throughout the world sharing his success principles and life-enhancing realizations with thousands of audiences, totaling over 1,000,000 people from all walks of life.

Jim has served as a success counselor to over 300 corporations worldwide. He was recently named as one of the world's top 20 success coaches and presented with the best of the best award out of the top 100 contributors of all time to the direct selling industry. He also mentored/coached Anthony Robbins for his first five years in business.

Jim is more than aware of the challenges we all face in making adaptive changes for a sustainable future.

Commitment

By Jim Britt

If you want real transformation or accomplishment in anything you do in life, then it comes down to one simple question you have to HONESTLY answer: Are you committed or merely interested and giving it a try? Most aren't serious about creating what they say they want, so they just dabble. It takes a commitment to yourself and in what you want if you want more of what life has to offer! Remember: You can do anything, IF you make the commitment to do it!

The quality of a person's life is in direct proportion to their commitment level, regardless of their chosen field of endeavor or what they want to accomplish.

And commitment only comes in one level and that's 100%. So look at it this way. Whatever you have in your life right now you have been 100% committed to having it…positive or not.

OK, so let's look at the positive. You've taken time to dream about what you want. You've started exploring your passion. You've even begun to set goals for yourself. Now it's time to take seriously your efforts to succeed.

Success at anything takes 100% commitment, otherwise you are still just "wishin and dreamin."

A commitment to do something is not a goal, but rather a decision. Decision comes first, and then the answers on how to accomplish it. Decision comes first, then the goals are the incremental steps to getting there.

Success takes time too. To experience success in any area of your life, you have to be able to push past life's road blocks and commit to not quit!

Focus your thoughts, intention, and energy on the prize you seek, not the challenges you face. Focus on the spot where you want to land, not the obstacles in the path.

One of my favorite remedies for the tough times is saying aloud, "I will not be defeated and I will not quit. I will do no less than whatever it takes to win!"

Commitment requires discipline. If you've made a commitment to yourself or to someone else, it'll require discipline to fulfill that promise, discipline to stay on track despite distractions and obstacles.

Not only will discipline help you reach your goals, but you'll feel better about yourself in the process.

Commitment is aided in part by routine. Commit to spending a certain amount of time each day on your goals or to focus on a project that brings you closer to reaching that goal.

Use your most creative time of day to work on your greatest challenges.

For some, that's early morning, before the day's events interfere.

Some are most creative and energetic in the afternoon. Others prefer the quiet of evening. Personally, I love the early mornings before anyone else is even out of bed.

Whatever works for you, if you'll make it a routine, it will soon become a habit. Only the habit of commitment will carry you to success.

Commitment can require making tough decisions, too. If you spend time making the tough decisions, you won't have it to spend time somewhere else where it doesn't matter. When faced with a tough decision, oftentimes we want to focus on tension-relieving decisions hoping the big one will take care of itself. Make the big decisions as they come up so you don't spend vital energy on things that do not matter.

The same is true with your talents and energy. Use your internal check to decide where to commit yourself to use your talents and energy. What goals are most important for your well-being and success?

Find ways to say "NO" to the things and people who drain you of your energy and efforts. There are so many distractions in today's world that will pull you off track if you let them. Ask yourself often, "Is this goal achieving or simply tension relieving?"

Here are some commitment helpers to keep you on track.

Put it on paper. If you'll commit to writing out your goals, ideas, and dreams as a commitment, you automatically give them more power in your mind.

I'm not talking about simply making a list of goals you want to accomplish. I'm talking about writing them down with a commitment attached. I am committed to earning $300,000 this year and I will do no less than whatever it takes to get there."

…or whatever…

Broaden your vision. Visualize the results you want. Use your imagination to 'feel' the results of what you are striving for and let it light the fire in your gut that will create the passion needed to carry you to the end result. Broaden your vision. What is possible? Get excited and filled with passion about what you want.

Imagination is a powerful tool. It connects your head with your heart and reinforces your commitment to the goal and gives you strength to continue.

Narrow your focus. Your goals are the steps you take to reach your ultimate decision that you are committed to accomplishing. Narrow your focus down to what you can do right now, today, this moment, that will move you closer to your goal. Set small goals that lead you down that 'yellow brick road' to your success.

It's easy to do little bits! Like adding water to a glass one drop at a time, your efforts will eventually overflow.

Do something daily. Don't go to bed without having done SOMETHING that will lead to the commitment you made to yourself.

Always give your best. Whatever you are doing, you have two choices. Give it a try and see what happens or to give it your very best. It doesn't mean you have to be "The best," but just give it YOUR best.

Excellence is always recognizable. Your commitment to excellence at every level will lead to the success you seek. It will draw people, events, and resources toward you.

Remember, how you show up in the world is how the world will show up for you. How you show up to others will be how others will show up to support you.

Time does not wait for you to commit to your success. It just ruthlessly passes you by. And when it's gone, it's gone forever! Only you can decide whether to be your best or mediocre with the time you have.

Hang on to your attitude and determination to succeed. Be patient with yourself, the people around you, and the process required to become successful. You attitude is the command post, the steering mechanism that will lead you where you want to go. Attitude says "I'll give it my best effort, or I'll give it a try and see what happens." Attitude will turn on or shut off the flow of ideas you need to guide you to your destination.

Take responsibility. In this world of instant gratification, high speed technology, and a 'quick fix' mentality, it seems that many people are no longer taking responsibility for taking care of themselves or for the results they produce and do not strive to be their very best. This is evidenced by increased social media addiction, the proliferation of health conditions, the rise in drug and alcohol abuse, and even the number of stress-related illnesses that take their toll every year.

Fix yourself. I have worked with many people over the years who ask, "Can you fix me?" My response is always the same. "I don't have a magic wand and I cannot make you do anything that you do not want to do." Nobody can fix you. You have to fix you. You have to take responsibility for you. I can offer suggestions and possible insights and strategies, but it is up to you whether you take responsibility and follow those guidelines.

I may be able to guide people to their inner awareness, to that place inside where they can see the truth about how they ended up where they are. I can offer suggestions that can help them implement change. The rest is up to them. If they want to change, they must make a personal commitment to do the work necessary to achieve the end result. People must have a desire for change and growth in their lives, and a commitment to follow through until it happens if they want change to happen.

Let's say you have a desire to lose a few pounds and you make the commitment to do so. Then the next day, you stop off to have lunch at a fast food place. That's not a commitment—it's just wishful thinking. Nobody can help you with that. If you want change, you have to commit to it. And nobody can do it for you.

Many people know something is wrong or lacking in their lives, but they are so out of touch with the truth about what got them where they are that they don't know how to change. Some I've worked with can't even verbalized what's wrong. They may say, "I just can't put my finger on it" or something similar. Most are quite clear about what they *don't* want, but in many cases have no real idea about what they *do* want. It is this dilemma that leads to confusion and inaction. Even when they believe they are clear and say they want to find their true purpose in life, or they feel stuck financially, it is most often something much deeper that emerges once the 'inner' work begins.

Unfortunately, many people fear delving too deeply and do not really want to change.

They a comfortable with who they are, and at the same time they hate who they are. This can show up as a myriad of excuses and self-sabotage so they can justify to themselves and others that they have to stay where they are. In reality, we all weigh out the pain of changing vs the pain of staying where we are. The lesser pain always wins out.

Change is frightening to many, because people are creatures of habit and prefer what is familiar, even when it is counter-productive to what they say they want. For example, a person weighing 200 pounds may 'say' "I want to get down to 150" and then proceed to 'do' everything to sabotage getting those results. They may continue to overeat at mealtime, sit in front of the TV or computer snacking all day, or just never get around to exercising.

Others say they want to become financially successful or get rich. But at the same time, just give them a beer and the TV remote and point them toward the TV and sofa and they'll complacently live out their life while complaining about their life. This is the attitude of so many today. You don't have to believe me, just take a look around.

The reason(s) for the disruption between intention and reality are usually deeply rooted in subconscious programming. That's what needs to be addressed to produce lasting change. It is the conscious mind that 'says' what is wanted or desired, but it is the subconscious where habits, behaviors, and emotions are housed and therefore, where the blockages need to be cleared. Until both parts of the mind are in alignment, any changes that are accomplished are generally short term.

Have you ever known someone that earns a lot of money, then spends like crazy until they are broke and struggling again? The reason is simply that they sink back into the familiar based on past programming. And the more they do it, the more it strengthens the programs. In fact, almost anything that you want to change in your life is likely to be facilitated by this inner work to change one's programming.

Do you ever wonder how it is that some people are able to take an idea and just run with it? How is it that they pull thousands of little things together to make one big idea work?

It all begins with two things. First is boldness. You have to be bold enough to step to center stage and put yourself in the spotlight. You can't be wimpy about what it is you want to do. No one else is going to shine that spotlight on you. If you want great things in life, you have to step into the spotlight.

Boldness requires that you have to take some risks. It means that you begin to act on a belief without all the facts. Boldness is the ability to withstand the ridicule or disbelief of others. Having boldness means having courage. And that means that you can step out on a journey with the belief that you can do something and know that when you do, things will begin to fall into place. Boldness is saying "YES" and then figuring out how.

Commitment is the second part of the equation. Many people are willing to make the decision to be bold and take risks, but not many are willing to stick with the decision until they reach their destination. With no commitment and follow-through, there is only dreaming…a fleeting thought. Without commitment, an idea will simply die in your mind.

When you accomplish anything, if you connect the dots backwards to where the original thought originated, you'll see boldness and commitment were the foundational ingredients to make it happen.

What was your last idea that you put aside? Was it something that came to you in the wee hours of the morning? Did you write it down, think on it, expand on the possibilities, dream of the results, and then lose your nerve or were you bold and committed to make it happen?

The Change[8]

Or possibly it was a fleeting moment of inspiration and then later you saw that someone had the same idea and acted upon it, and the idea grew into a huge success?

How often have you lost your nerve and your boldness faded, or after stepping into the spotlight you lost the commitment to make it happen?

Did you know that every time you have an idea, the law of probabilities says that ten other people have the same idea? The person who has the success with the idea is the person who acts upon it first and fastest and sticks with it. This requires boldness and commitment.

All creation begins with an idea. But how do you start? Take the first step. Write it down and consider all the possibilities. Contemplate and let the idea grow. Get caught up in the moment. Let it run away with you. Let the idea carry you away to a place you have never been. How would it feel if this or that happened? Let it work its magic on your emotions. Could it be successful? Play the "what if" game with the idea. You will never know what lies ahead unless you decide, be bold, commit and take the first step, and then stick with it until it's done.

Successful people often try and fail. But without the boldness, commitment, and taking the first step, they would never succeed either. Do not be afraid of failure. It's a key part of succeeding at anything. If you fail at something, it doesn't mean it won't work. It simply means you approached it incorrectly. Be bold. Embrace your fear head-on. Fear is simply a made-up story of something that hasn't even happened. It is not real. Remind yourself again and again, nothing ventured, nothing gained. Then make the commitment to do no less than wherever it will take to accomplish your goal. When others see your daring, your boldness, and your commitment to follow through, their respect and belief in you also grows. Remember, how you show up to the world is how those in the world show up to support you.

So go ahead! Decide what you REALLY want! Be bold! Make the commitment and take action toward what you want. Your destiny awaits!

Commitment: "That extra resource you draw upon when the going gets tough."

Jim Britt

www.JimBritt.com

www.PowerOfLettingGo.com

www.CrackingTheRichCode.com

www.FaceBook.com/JimBrittOnline

www.JourneyBeginsNow.com

Jim Lutes

Having taught his branded form of human performance since the early 1990s, Mr. Lutes has accelerated top level entrepreneurs throughout his career by conducting trainings on personal growth and subconscious programming into worldwide markets.

During this time, Jim took his skills regarding the human mind, and combining it with trainings on influence, persuasion, and communication strategies, he launched Lutes International in the early 1990s. Based in San Diego, California, Jim has taught seminars for corporations, sales forces, individuals, and athletes. Having appeared on television, radio, and worldwide stages, Jim's style, knowledge, and effectiveness provide profound results.

"Jim Lutes possesses a unique ability to create performance change in an individual in a fraction of the time it takes his competitors." The core of humans decisions are based on the programs we acquire, reinforce, and grow. Combining Jim's various trainings, individuals can reach new levels of achievement and fulfillment in all areas of life. The results are at times nothing short of astonishing.

Universal Laws and Rules of the Mind

By Jim Lutes

Many of you may have heard of the twelve Universal Laws. For sure, you will have heard of the Law of Attraction, since it has become wildly popularized through books and film over the last few years. Many of you may have experienced programs or personal development books that suggest success through using the Universal Laws. Still others of you may have found that it wasn't that simple, and the Universal Laws were not effective in the practical application you tried. Throughout my years of working in personal development, I have come up with my own Eight Rules of the Mind. What I have observed through implementation of the Eight Rules is this: If you apply my Eight Rules of the Mind with the Universal Laws, you will activate their power and thereby turbo-charge your own capability to make manifest all that you desire. Applying the Universal Laws with the Eight Rules of the Mind at a deeper level will serve to amplify their power and effectiveness in your life.

Just like there is a virtually universal way to get in shape, and that is to exercise regularly, so there is a universal way to access the world's abundance. The latter involves knowing and using the Universal Laws. Now, just as there are a million different ways to exercise, and some people believe Crossfit or P90X are the most effective ways of training the body, I believe that combining my Eight Rules of the Mind with the Universal Laws is like doing Crossfit AND P90X daily to get in shape! It's a double whammy of powerful techniques to retrain your subconscious mind.

There are twelve Universal Laws. In brief, these laws are:

The Law of Divine Oneness. This law is the foundation of the Universal Laws, and is about the interconnectedness of everything within the universe. Just as I have mentioned previously how the subconscious mind is the access point to this Universal Power, so this law serves to back up the idea that all energy comes from this place of Universal Power. This law also is about how what we think, say, and do affects everyone and everything around us.

The Law of Vibration. This law is about how everything in the universe moves and vibrates. Each thing, each sound, and even each thought has its own vibrational frequency. These vibrational frequencies move in spiral patterns. If you take a good close look at some of the beauty of nature, you will start to see these spiral patterns everywhere.

The Law of Action. This law is about generating action to support your thoughts and dreams and it must be undertaken to achieve any physical manifestation of thoughts, dreams, or goals. However, this law suggests that once action is taken, this law comes into effect to ensure the dreams and goals come to fruition.

The Law of Correspondence. This law is about how physics, particularly quantum physics, accounts for all the energy, light, vibration and motion experienced in the physical world and their counterparts in the energetic realm.

The Law of Cause and Effect. This law translates simply as, "Every action has a reaction." This law is also commonly matched to the concept of 'karma.' Basically, if you are mean to someone and they are mean to you in return, you are experiencing the Law of Cause and Effect.

The Law of Compensation. This law applies the Law of Cause and Effect to allow for abundance to come to those in response to acts of giving, expressions of gratitude, or other charitable actions taken. The abundance or gifts that are received come in direct relation with the acts of giving that have occurred. For good or bad, that which you give is returned. When you are angry, you will encounter others who are angry. When you are generous and giving, you will be sure to receive.

The Law of Attraction. Simply put, this law states that, "Like attracts like," whether in our thoughts or our actions. We draw that which we think of to us, like a magnetic attraction. This is the most talked-about and popular of the laws, in use by numerous people in the personal development field to help people manifest their desires.

The Law of Perpetual Transmutation of Energy. This law is about the potential we have to change the energy, or vibrational output, in our lives by recognizing that there are higher and lower vibrations. Applying this law along with skilled use of energies and vibrations allows us to shift energy and effect change in our lives. On a practical level, an example of this is how you choose to respond to people that annoy you at work; someone using this law will choose to respond with love and compassion, regardless of the annoyance, knowing that their response will allow them to feel better about the situation, and accepting the fact that they cannot control the people that annoy them.

The Law of Relativity. This law reveals that the problems we encounter as individuals and in our lifetimes are only as challenging as we need them to be; that we are only ever faced with that which we can handle and ultimately better ourselves for having learned from. This law also invites us to gauge our lives, and perceived problems in our lives, relative to one another.

The Law of Polarity. This law works with opposites. All things have an opposite – think of the sun and the moon, black and white, yin and yang. Applying this law on a practical level looks like choosing a positive thought to replace a negative thought to hold in your mind.

The Law of Rhythm. This law is about the universal rhythms that guide universal flow, through the seasons, and the human life cycle, for example. Everything is moving to its own rhythm.

The Law of Gender. This law is about creation, and the manifestation of all things in the masculine or the feminine.

Many of you have probably already heard of all of these Laws, especially the Law of Attraction. I'm not going to dive too much deeper into each law to explain how to make it work for you. What I am going to do, rather, is outline for you the Eight Rules of the Mind, and then match them up with what I perceive to be the corresponding Universal Law to maximize effectiveness in practice.

Here are the Eight Rules of the Mind:

Every thought or idea causes a physical reaction.

What is expected tends to be realized.

Imagination is more powerful than knowledge when dealing with your own mind or the mind of another.

Opposing ideas cannot be held at the same time.

Once an idea has been accepted by the subconscious, it remains until replaced by another idea. The longer it has been held, the more opposition there is to replacing it.

An emotionally induced symptom tends to cause organic change if persisted in long enough.

Each suggestion acted upon creates less opposition to successive suggestion.

When dealing with the subconscious mind and its functions, the greater the conscious effort, the less the subconscious response.

Let's look at these rules now within the context of the Universal Laws.

Rule number one: every thought or idea causes a physical reaction. This corresponds to the Universal Law of Cause and Effect. The Law of Cause and Effect reiterates that nothing happens by chance. Every action has a reaction, according to this law. If we take this further and merge it with my rule that specifies that not only does every action have a reaction, but that every thought or idea causes a physical reaction, we can start to see the truth behind the advice to watch our thoughts.

Basically, every thought that passes through your mind, whether generated consciously or subconsciously, will cause a physical reaction. For example, you might think to yourself "I want a new car." You work hard, you earn the money required, you go to the car dealership, you test drive a car, you buy a car, and soon enough, you have your new car. Regardless of how long it took between the thought and the reality of having that new car, the thought of "I want a new car" produced the new physical reality of you in a new car. Now, what if you find yourself suddenly wanting ice cream, without noticing that you had the thought that you want ice cream? Perhaps you watched a commercial or it is a hot day, and something triggered your subconscious mind to provoke that thought. This leads to you buying ice cream. Think back to times in your life when this has happened and you'll notice how every thought led to a physical reaction.

What is important to recognize about this is that the thought comes before the reaction. Pay attention to where you react, particularly when you have reacted without thinking, and chances are you were reacting out of a pattern generated by your subconscious. It makes no difference whether your thoughts are good or bad, but they will generate an effect on the physical body. There is the story of a woman who believed so wholeheartedly that she was pregnant that her hormones actually changed and her body physically manifested the power of that thought and belief. Thoughts are powerful, and this is the bottom line. Thoughts affect our physical reality, regardless from where the thought is generated. It is important to understand this first and foremost as one of the Rules of the Mind, so that you can start to fully grasp the power of the mind, both conscious and subconscious.

The next Rule of the Mind is this: What is expected tends to be realized. This is in line with the Universal Law of Attraction. The Law of Attraction is all about how we create the events that surround us in life. This law suggests that like attracts like; that is, if you are constantly struggling and your mindset is focused on the struggle, then you will only serve to generate more struggle. It also means that if you are focused on the positive and seeing the world as abundant, then you will generate positive thoughts and abundance. The way I see it, with this rule, your thoughts hold expectation and whatever it is you expect, consciously or not, will come to be present in your reality. If you expect to be in poor health, you will be in poor health. If you expect to be wealthy, you will be wealthy.

This law is an insidious cancer on the negative, but a powerful force on the positive for those who really get it. The brain responds to images, regardless of whether these images were internally or externally generated. This means there is unlimited potential within each of us to either manifest all the positive things we want, or crash and burn. Do you expect to be in good shape and good health, with a flourishing business and loving, healthy relationships? Do you expect everything that you touch to fail, and a life of pain and misery awaiting you? This is the power within this law. If you expect the doom, you will realize the doom. If you expect goodness, you will receive goodness. Once you reprogram your mind so your subconscious is not keeping you in old patterns that have you expecting what you've perhaps already had for your whole life – misery, misfortune, you name it – then you can step into this law more fully, knowing that what you expect, you realize.

The third Rule of the Mind states that imagination is more powerful than knowledge when dealing with your own mind or the mind of another. This is also congruent with the Law of Attraction, particularly when we consider that the subconscious mind responds to visuals and images. In our world today, where we are literally saturated by images suggesting things to us all day, every day, it is important to continue the work of visualization in order to achieve your dreams. To visualize and imagine what it is you are wanting will help you create it much faster, as this is the language the subconscious mind can respond to. What you watch and the images you take in affect you too, so be mindful about what you choose to look at. When you watch violent TV shows or look at images of things you don't want, your mind is not registering these things as good or bad, but the images are coming in regardless. Selecting, with discernment, the images that you hold in your mind is one of the keys to drawing your dreams closer. Try to shut out or at the very least limit the images and media that do not contribute to your desired 'big picture' result.

While you cannot control every image that is presented to you, it is again important to be aware of the images you hold in your mind. For example, consider the salesman who has a brand new product and a warehouse full of stock and he is excited to sell. There he is, the proverbial 'shingle' hung out, and no one buys anything on his first day of business. Now the salesman has a choice. He could imagine nothing but failure and picture his warehouse closed and locked for good, his sad shingle falling by the wayside. Or, the salesman could imagine wild success, his products flying off the shelves, and not interpret how his first day went as the harbinger of certain doom. Either way, it is in the salesman's control what image he wants to send to his subconscious mind to generate a physical reality. Consider how you respond to the ups and downs of life, and watch what your imagination creates.

The fourth Rule of the Mind is that two opposing ideas cannot be held at the same time. This is linked with the Law of Polarity. The Law of Polarity states that everything has an opposite. Knowing that everything has an opposite, we can then eliminate the negative thoughts we experience by concentrating on positive thoughts in their place. This is a valuable law to understand, because within this concept is the real root of the work of reprogramming your mind. If you catch yourself thinking a negative thought like "I'm so broke," you cannot think "I'm so rich" simultaneously. However, if you catch yourself with the negative thought, and quickly shift to the positive thought, you have in that moment made a conscious choice to hold on to an idea that supports you, not erodes you. Think of your mind as a nightclub. Sometimes when your nightclub is occupied with negative thoughts, it feels like a burden. But there are people out there who don't feel this as a burden, because they have used the "bouncer" to repopulate their nightclubs with positive thoughts, knowing that the nightclub cannot entertain both types of thoughts at the same time. Applying this rule in a practical sense requires being aware of your thoughts at all times, and consciously canceling out the negative thoughts to replace positive ones. This means that you can no longer float through your day feeling like you don't know why things are happening like they are. The more present you can become to the thoughts that sabotage you throughout each day, the more you will be able to catch them and replace them with thoughts that lift you.

The next rule of the mind is as follows: Once an idea has been accepted by the subconscious mind, it remains until replaced by another idea. The longer it has been held, the more opposition there is to replacing it. Again, the Law of Polarity is at work through this rule. This is essentially the repopulating of the nightclub. Once you decide to reprogram your mind so that your subconscious mind no longer controls you with its limiting and unsupportive patterns, it will be an effort to replace these thoughts with positive ones. Your subconscious mind will put up a great fight because it believes it knows best and is protecting you. A struggle will be presented. After all, a lot of the patterns running from your subconscious mind were survival mechanisms formed from your childhood to keep you safe and assure your needs were met. You bet it has dug in its heels! However, if it is limiting you in your present life and you know you want to transform your life into the rich and aligned life it could be, then you will have to work day in and day out to reprogram your mind. This is not to say "don't do it"—far from it. Rather, this is just to allow you to understand that the subconscious mind will give some push-back at the beginning as you repopulate the nightclub. The key point to focus on in this rule is that the subconscious mind accepts ideas from the conscious mind, and that these ideas can be replaced. I am saying that you take this one step deeper in your personal work, and seek to replace these ideas with the right techniques in order to create lasting change at the level required.

Rule of the Mind number six is this: An emotionally induced symptom tends to cause organic change if persisted in long enough. This loosely corresponds with the Law of Perpetual Transmutation of Energy. This Law reminds us that we all have the power to change within us. We can strive to operate from that place of our highest selves and stop operating from ego or limiting identity. If we apply this rule of the mind, backed up by the Law of Perpetual Transmutation of Energy, we can effect change at a profound level in our lives. This rule of the mind invites us to go beyond just thought and get to the emotion behind the thought. For example, think about how you react every time you receive a bill that is more than you were anticipating. For a lot of you, you might react with anxiety or stress, regardless of whether or not you have the funds to pay the bill. Have you wondered where the anxiety or stress have come from? More often than not, the anxiety around paying a bill has nothing to do with the physical work of paying the bill. Even a millionaire could be subject to feeling anxiety when faced with a large bill. The anxiety is the emotion associated with the act of paying bills. Wouldn't it be nice to change that? This rule is an invitation to grow awareness of how you respond emotionally to things. The awareness then gives you access to changing your emotion. You no longer need to default to anxiety if you get present to what is really happening. If you are delighted with your life—it's your daughter's wedding day—your emotional state is genuinely happy and loving, then you get a bill and feel anxious all of a sudden, what emotion is more authentic? The happy and loving emotions, of course. The anxiety popping up is learned, and not reflective of your present truth in that moment. This is how you know which emotions are coming out of programming in the subconscious mind and which are really real for you in each moment. Chances are, some of the emotions that don't feel so great are ones that you don't even know where they came from. Just like you can work on flipping your negative thoughts into positive thoughts, so with this rule can you work on dispelling emotions that grip and sabotage you, carried over from your subconscious, to make room for actual authentic emotions that serve you. Implementing this rule gets you present to what is actually happening emotionally in each moment, versus what is a manufactured emotion brought up by the subconscious mind.

The next Rule of the Mind states that each suggestion acted upon creates less opposition to successive suggestion. This is reflected in the Law of Rhythm. Everything in the universe has its own rhythm – think of the seasons, or even our own life cycles as humans. As we grow more aligned with the universe, so we see where we can avoid wasting our time on inconsequential or self-sabotaging thoughts and behaviors. As you evolve, and start to suggest new possibilities to your subconscious mind, you will see it only becomes easier over time. As you begin the work of repopulating your nightclub and bringing more positive thoughts into your mind, your subconscious mind will loosen its grip on the long-held thoughts and beliefs, and be more receptive to the new suggestions you are giving it. Recall that the subconscious mind is highly susceptible to suggestion, which is why the reprogramming techniques I am sharing with you are so effective.

Finally, the last Rule of the Mind states that when dealing with the subconscious mind and its functions, the greater the conscious effort, the lesser the subconscious response. This again works along the lines of the Law of Perpetual Transmutation of Energy. Energy is constantly shifting; no matter how stuck we feel, we are actually in a constant state of change. Our cells are repeatedly dying and being born, air is moving in and out of our lungs, our bodies are undertaking hundreds of bodily functions in each moment. As we apply the Rules of the Mind in concert with the Universal Laws, we begin moving out of being programmed human beings whose subconscious minds are running the show and into conscious individuals making choices in real time with full awareness. This is true empowerment.

To contact Jim:

Email: info@lutesinternational.com

Websites: www.lutesinternational.com

www.jimluteslive.com

Valerie Bernard

Valerie Bernard is a Certified Coach, Trainer, Speaker, and co-author of Work Smarter Not Harder and Transformational Leadership. She is sought after for her expertise in intentional leadership coaching. She is founder and CEO of Executive Training Centers Inc. Since 2002, she has earned her stellar reputation by enhancing the performance of every organization she serves. High-energy, entertaining, and educational are words used to describe Valerie's presentations. Her combination of expertise, humor, and inspiration energizes people to take action in both their personal and business lives.

Bernard inspires big thinking, decisive action, and welcome results whether she is addressing groups of 12 mastermind team members or convention audiences of 5000. Valerie's leadership workshops deepen understanding about relationships and organizational systems. She is committed to transforming organizational leadership gaps into powerful performance advantages. Valerie is described by her clients as engaging, persuasive, and game changing for their organizations.

Valerie is the performance improvement specialist HR executives engage to assess current situations, create stronger team collaborations, and bring about improved performance. She turns stressful situations into systematic, reliable performance improvements that give decision makers cause for celebration.

Bernard earned her Master's Degree at Marshall University in Huntington, West Virginia. She intends to complete work on her Ph.D. in Human Performance Improvement from Capella University in December 2015.

The Biggest Game-CHANGER

By Valerie Bernard

"Life is change. Growth is optional. Choose wisely." *Unknown*

The biggest game-CHANGER is about having an open mind to all the opportunities which come our way when accepting change as a part of the process for learning, growing, and developing to become the very best YOU can be in all areas of your life. In Series 6, we touched upon six game-changing principles to consider when facing or implementing change. In Series 7, we touched upon a basic understanding of theories, models, tools, and techniques to provide you with a powerful opportunity to move an organization toward expanding the focus toward performance improvement when implementing change initiatives. I mentioned I would be expanding on this in *The Change, Series 8*. If you have not reviewed these two books in the series (*The Change*[6] & *The Change*[7]), I would encourage you to get a copy, take some time to relax, and review the chapters. It should not take you more than 30 minutes, and I am confident you will have at least one-takeaway making this worth your time!

After thinking about the direction for my contribution to *The Change*[8], and after suggesting I would expand on the theories, models, tools, and techniques in *The Change*[8], well...I decided to CHANGE. I am sure you will not be disappointed at the direction of this Chapter, as it could apply to both your personal and professional lives. With your permission, I would like to start with a story about my father, Van Bernard. I encourage you to continue, as the second part of the Chapter will focus on *Embracing the Seven Game-Changing Principles of a Transformational Leader.*

January 15, 2009 11:11 p.m.

Point Pleasant, West Virginia

My mind was a jumble of confused thoughts and dragging weariness, still hoping it all wasn't true. But, as I sighed deeply, I knew it was. My father was gone. The combination of pain, loss, and disbelief, on top of my utter state of exhaustion, left me in a state of numbness. Just an hour before my father's death, he had given me a list of things he wanted me to do for my mom. The first thing Dad requested was for me to go to Lowe's on Saturday morning to get a specific kind of salt for their driveway. He knew exactly what he wanted me to get, and he was specific I should do this first thing Saturday morning. Secondly, Dad told me "code" is not always a bad thing. There were many times in the previous two years my father had coded, and I told him on this evening I hated to hear this word. The last thing Dad shared with me was to look for yellow butterflies, and I would know he would be close by. He gave me a beautiful gift on this night; however, I did not realize the magnitude of the gift at this time. After reviewing the list with me, my father died unexpectedly from a ruptured stomach aneurism one hour later.

While my mom and I sat in the emergency room in shock and disbelief, I held tightly to the list of things Dad needed me to get done for him.

The list…I now needed to get started. The first thing was the trip to Lowes to get the salt.

January 16, 2009 8:30 a.m.

I dressed quickly and walked into the kitchen where my mother sat dealing with her own grief and pain. She had spent fifty-four years with one man. I couldn't even fathom something like this.

Mom looked at me and said, "Where are you going?"

"To Lowe's. To get the salt Dad wanted."

Mom looked at me with disbelief. "Your dad wouldn't want you out on the roads. You need to stay home, and we need to go to the funeral home."

"No, Mom. If Dad said to do it, I'm going to do it." Mom looked away because she knew once I got something in my head, it was happening.

Without another word, I bundled up and headed out into the snow to my car. I was heading to Lowe's, which was an hour away. The driving conditions were not good. Living in West Virginia, I had become accustomed to it.

Somehow—by the grace of God—through icy roads, I made it to Lowe's. It was barely 10 a.m. Once I was inside, I dried my tears a final time, took a deep breath, and set my determined mind for some help.

I saw a lady at a counter. "Excuse me, but I'm looking for a special brand of salt. The kind that doesn't pit your driveway. Can you please direct me?"

She looked at me and said, "Let me get you some help."

"May I help you ma'am?" His tag spelled out the name Kyle.

The Change[8]

"Yes, Kyle; I need this special kind of salt. I have it written down here."

I stood there as he punched some keys and stared at the screen. "Well, it says we have two bags in inventory."

"Sure, I'll take them."

"Okay, they should be in Aisle 15."

An hour later, after we had covered every aisle twice, Kyle turned to me and said, "Ma'am, I just can't find it. The computer says they're here…but I don't know where."

I blinked trying to hold back the sting of tears. "I cannot leave. You don't understand. I have got to find it."

Kyle looked at me and said, "Ma'am…are you crying?"

I replied, "Well, I just lost my dad last night. He gave me this list of things…I'm supposed to get this salt."

His eyes widened, "Lady, have you looked outside?"

"As a matter of fact I have, Kyle. There's about ten inches of snow on the ground."

"It's January in West Virginia. You think you're gonna being seeing a yellow butterfly?"

"As a matter of fact I do because my dad gave me this list, and he told me to be looking for the yellow butterflies."

Kyle decided the woman in front of him was not going to be easy to get rid of. "I guess if we're gonna see butterflies, we need to go outside. But I can tell you there's no salt outside. The only thing we have out in the garden center is mulch and potting soil."

I wiped my tears and with a mournful voice said, "Do you mind if we go look?"

"Sure lady, whatever you want."

We began walking side by side and I said, "Kyle, you believe in God, don't you? You believe in heaven?"

"Yeah."

"You believe God could send a butterfly? If there's supposed to be a butterfly, we're gonna see it...even in the winter, right?"

"Well, yeah, I guess so."

When we reached the garden center, there were bags of mulch and dirt stacked everywhere. Snow covered the tops of the bags. Flakes of snow drifting down lazily, Kyle stood next to me realizing how hopeless this was.

I chuckled as I said, "My dad really has a sense of humor too. This is an example of it."

Then something in the corner caught Kyle's attention and he spun to face it directly. "Lady!" he said as he nudged me with his elbow before pointing to a spot about six feet off the ground.

I followed his arm to the biggest yellow butterfly I had ever seen. We both stood mesmerized as this butterfly drifted over and landed on a stack of mulch in the corner of the garden center. Kyle coughed out a low question, "...Y-you think the salt is in that pallet of mulch?"

I smiled, feeling tiny rivers of frozen tears crack on my cheeks. "Yes, I really do. Can we get it?"

The Change[8]

After 45 minutes of moving various stacks around with the forklift, he climbed off the machine and stared at two bags at the bottom of the pallet. The yellow butterfly had landed on this stack. "I can't believe this…but here's the two bags. These two must have been left over from last year because this mulch came in during the summer. Wow! Unbelievable!"

After a minute or so, Kyle loaded up my cart with two bags of the special salt Dad wanted me to buy. Once he had helped me push the cart through the snow into the store, he said, "Okay…you're on your own now."

"No, I think I still have plenty of help."

He smiled and then disappeared. I continued on, making my way to the checkout.

It didn't take long to realize there was no one at any of the registers. I pushed the cart up to the customer service counter and said, "Can I go ahead and check out? I have the bags of salt."

The girl who had first helped me stared at me in amazement. "Why, you're still here?!"

"Yes," I said. "And I'm just ready to check out now. I need to get back to my mom."

The girl picked up a phone and suddenly, her voice boomed over the store's loudspeakers. "Code to register one."

Instantly I shuddered. Code was a word I hated because my dad had coded several times in the hospital. To hear it in Lowe's—

"Code to register one?" I said, "What does that mean?"

She looked at me casually and said, "That means hurry up and get to your register."

There on line three of the list my dad gave me was the following: *Code does not always mean a bad thing.* I felt my body relax. I began talking to myself.

Code does not always mean a bad thing.

A minute later, a young girl slid in behind one of the registers. As she was getting a Lowe's vest on, I looked at her shirt…it had the prettiest yellow butterfly embroidered on the front.

"Why are you wearing butterflies?"

She smiled and said, "I just love butterflies. It reminds me there's a heaven."

A smile diverted the tears around my lips. "What is your name?"

I watched as she took it out of the vest pocket and pinned it on. When I saw it, I looked up to heaven and smiled at Dad. I knew everything was going to be alright.

Her name was Angel.

The story continues in another book at another time in the future, but I wanted to share the short version of this story to illustrate loss is a very hard change. Thinking of the gift of the yellow butterfly helped me move from the familiar to the unfamiliar. It was a shift in thinking. Everyone faces a time, most likely more than once, where a transition is difficult. Combining personal experiences with professional experiences, I have been able to learn about transformation in a way I never thought of before the yellow butterfly. Thank you, Dad, for this gift, and for teaching me about leadership and life.

Could I share with you some principles I learned from my father regarding transformational leadership?

Embracing the Seven Game-Changing Principles of a Transformational Leader

"What the caterpillar calls the end of the world, the rest of the world calls the butterfly." –Richard Bach

In the beginning of my career many years ago, I assumed "leadership" as an activity was pretty much equally applied across organizations and cultures. I have since learned different cultures and personalities require leadership unique to them. If the success and growth of others are the responsibility of a leader, this truth cannot be forgotten. Paying attention to the uniqueness will influence attitudes and behaviors and positively expand the limits of each individual in the workplace, including myself. The second part of this chapter highlights some similarities between leadership and the transformation of a caterpillar into a butterfly. The development of butterflies is a complex process that in the end turns out to be something very different from the beginning.

Game-CHANGING Principle #1 – Vision

When the caterpillar first created his cocoon, the caterpillar did not know what was happening. The caterpillar was closed off from the old world, but not yet ready to enter the new world.

A vision is a result you picture. For some, that picture represents a purpose and an accompanying set of values necessary for achieving it. For others, vision represents the horror of change. Norman Vincent Peale said, "If you want to get somewhere you have to know where you want to go and how to get there." There will be obstacles. Vision helps in overcoming obstacles. It can show what path the organization should pursue. Any routines and processes which do not support the vision should be reevaluated.

The metamorphosis which the caterpillar must undergo to transform the caterpillar to butterfly is very painful, but unless he endures the metamorphosis, he cannot become the butterfly. The caterpillar has no idea what to expect. As the metamorphosis progresses, the caterpillar slowly starts to understand what is happening.

Key point: Transformational leaders turn challenges into opportunities in the pursuit of their shared vision.

Game-CHANGING Principle #2 – Focus

Can the caterpillar really imagine what his new existence would be like? If the caterpillar told the other caterpillars what was going to happen, most of them would think he was insane.

Does this happen to leaders who try to explain the vision? Yes. As leaders, we see the big picture. We see the horizon. And possibly beyond. Our vision helps us see what direction to take. Add to it our focus, which is what keeps us on the right road heading toward our destination.

It takes the varied talents of the people on your team. Sometimes individuals do not see how their strengths can help the team reach the goals. As a leader, you must help them recognize their strengths, develop them, and focus application of them on reaching the goals. One necessary ingredient for you to lead people in recognizing their strengths is for you to praise their abilities. This reinforces them and helps build a bond of trust between leader and staff.

If we as leaders are not clear about the direction we are going, we cannot lead with clarity and decisiveness. Without a clear focus, we impose our beliefs on those we lead, instead of motivating them toward a shared goal.

Key point: Transformational leaders focus on the positive opportunities to change the world.

Game-CHANGING Principle #3 – Courage

Regardless of how hard the butterfly tries, it cannot possibly fly until it first discards the cocoon. Before it can fly, the butterfly must force its way out of the cocoon, which takes some effort.

Courage is the strength to act on strong beliefs, whatever the risk. When leaders remain true in their adherence to guiding principles, regardless of opposition, they generate confidence and strength, a necessary platform for building success. As Winston Churchill stated, "Courage is the first of human qualities because it is the quality which guarantees all others." It takes courage to get past the disappointments—trust me, disappointments are inevitable.

Courage can manifest itself in different ways in the workplace. Sometimes, simply disagreeing is an act of courage in itself. As a new leader, rocking the status quo requires tapping into your courage. It takes courage to present outside-the-norm ideas. Talking about values, vision, and purpose and holding on to the vision and focusing on the task at hand is one way to turn fear into courage. Although I have many times heard responses such as "not right now," "maybe you should slow down," and "we have never done it that way before," with persistence and enthusiasm, I have been able to share my vision by having the courage to take risks. You can do this too!

Key point: Transformational leaders have the courage to take risks.

Game-CHANGING Principle #4 – Choice

The butterfly recalled he had worried about which caterpillar had the juiciest leaf, and whether the leaves would always be there. The butterfly now sees the trees and knows there are other trees.

Making the choice is the first step. Everything else follows from the choices we make. To choose a direction is to commit ourselves to it in spite of all the reasons why others say the particular choice is not doable. It means accepting the risk that focusing on the choice entails. Growth is not possible without risk. It is not so much what happens as it is sticking to the choices you make.

Creating a culture that is about change and continuous improvement is one of the first decisions a leader will make. Helping individuals to build upon their talents and strengths is a great place to start. By asking open-ended questions about ideas your team members have for improvement, you may discover the fears of individual team members. Transformational synergy is created in this way. Giving team members the opportunity to make choices in crafting their own particular plans for professional development will result in extremely positive outcomes.

Key point: Transformational leaders make choices without looking back.

Game-CHANGING Principle #5 – Values

Two caterpillars are conversing and a beautiful butterfly floats by. One caterpillar turns and says to the other, "You'll never get me up on one of those butterfly things."—Scott Simmerman

There is a major lesson to learn from the caterpillar story as it applies to transformational leadership and vision. In order to manifest a vision for growth, we have to welcome the inevitability of change. What then do values have to do with leadership? Values serve as a beginning point for all employees of an organization. Values are fundamental to our identity. They are guides that dictate our choices for implementing the organizational vision.

Leaders of integrity makes decisions rooted in strongly held values. Leaders who embrace principles must not only set moral standards, but also effectively communicate a code of conduct to those they lead. As a transformational leader, always remain faithful to your core convictions. Martin Luther King, Jr. said it best when he stated, "The ultimate measure of man is not where he stands in moments of comfort and convenience, but where he stands at times of challenge and controversy."

Key point: Transformational leaders understand positive values endure.

Game-CHANGING Principle #6 – Empathy

The butterfly lands on the flower of a tree—the same tree the butterfly had lived on as the caterpillar. The butterfly carries pollen to another flower, to fertilize the seed, which will fall to the ground and grow into a tree for other caterpillars to live on.

Empathy is sensitivity to others' feelings and concerns. Empathetic leaders are sensitive to the differences in how people think and feel about things. The ability to evaluate the situation from another person's point of view best describes empathy. Understanding what your team, customers, and competition are going through is critical to transformational leadership. Empathy inspires people to stay with a leader when the going gets tough.

Sometimes, as I have discovered, we get so excited about our vision we sometimes forget about the feelings of the people we are trying to lead. The leader's goal is to listen. Listening is essential in every leadership position. Empathy can get lost in the shuffle of challenges and other situations in the workplace. Be careful not to let this happen.

Key point: Transformational leaders exercise empathy and understand the leader is a servant.

Game-CHANGING Principle #7 – Passion

We spend most of our lifetimes like a caterpillar struggling to survive and thinking only of our immediate needs. The metamorphosis which we undergo is extremely painful, but unless we endure the metamorphosis, we will remain as caterpillars. If we live with passion, we are like a butterfly gliding about and enjoying the true beauty of the world.

Do people rally around a passionate leader? Do people who are passionate about their work have a contagious enthusiasm which inspires others to follow? Yes! Effective leaders inspire and generate action. Leadership is not a position. Leadership is action! Passionate connections spark passionate responses.

Whom do you think about when I ask you about the greatest leaders of all times? John F. Kennedy? Churchill? Gandhi? Nelson Mandela? These leaders led their followers with fire and passion. Once a leader is committed to a vision and possesses a clear focus, along with the ability to take risks and to make choices based on values and empathy, passion kicks in. Hegel wrote, "Nothing great in the world has been accomplished without passion."

Key Point: Transformational leaders turn passion into action.

Summary

It would seem many organizations are trapped in a cocoon of their own making, unable to visualize what heights to which they can soar. Leaders who embrace vision, focus, courage, choice, value, empathy, and passion can transform mediocre organizations into high-performing organizations. At the heart of all transformation is the transformation of ourselves. Like the caterpillar to the butterfly, we are all at certain stages of progress in our leadership and in our lives. You may be at the beginning where ideas are born, but have not yet become a reality. You may be at the point at which you decide to take action. You may be developing an idea of changing direction. The symbol of the butterfly can remind you that transformation and change begin with you and leadership and life are a never-ending cycle of self-transformation.

"If nothing ever changed, there would be no butterflies."--Unknown

Dedicated to my father, Van William Bernard.

I am still seeing the yellow butterflies, and I will see you again one day soon.

To contact Valerie:

Executive Training Centers, Inc.

Post Office Box 433

Point Pleasant, WV 25550

Cell: 304.941.4653

Email: valerie@executivetraningcenters.com

Twitter: @ValerieBernard

Web: www.executivetrainingcenters.com

www.linkedin.com/in/executivetrainingcenters

Johnny Morney

Johnny Morney is a successful international businessman and an award-winning speaker and author. He has a clear-cut concept whereby just helping others with what is important to them ensures that you will attract the best that life has to offer to you. Presently through his world travels and massive network and relationships, Johnny has shared the stage and co-authored books with some of the sharpest minds of our time such as Les Brown, Johnny Wimbrey, Bryan Flanagan, John Di Lemme, Jack Canfield, Tony Robbins, Greg S. Reid, and Dr. Wayne Dyer, just to name a few. Johnny has furthermore founded the world's first elite, invitation-only international organization of today's fastest growing business owners, corporate movers and shakers, and entrepreneurs who quite literally want to make the world their playground. The organization is called the Point Of Connections. Just as LinkedIn and Facebook has changed connecting and the face of the business world, so will P.O.C.—it is the new Purple Cow. Johnny has been fortunate to have worked internationally with, and become friends with, some of the leading figures in the business, political, entertainment, media, and entrepreneurial worlds.

Top 5 Global Networking Positions of Power Factors

By Johnny Morney

When we think of powerful people, we often incorrectly equate power with fame. We believe that individuals we see in the media on a regular basis possess much of the decision-making power with regard to business, politics, media, and entertainment.

Yet, some of the most powerful individuals in the world are not often in the public eye. They do not consistently seek the limelight and are often absent from the public's view. They prefer to wield their power without the questions and scrutiny public exposure bring with them.

Their positions may be the result of entrepreneurial brilliance, nepotism and inheritance, or just plain good luck. However their influential status was achieved, they can affect the lives of a handful of people or they can impact millions. They can alter the way individuals communicate, develop new industries, and even elect presidents.

If your goal is to become one of these power brokers, it is important that you understand the five factors of global networking positions of power. As you build your financial empire, you'll need to keep these five positions in mind and utilize this information to shape your own destiny.

Position #1: The Godfather (The Don Corleone Factor)

The position of "godfather" is arguably the most powerful, yet least understood, power position in business. In the 1972 epic film *The Godfather*, Vito Corleone was the go-to person when the average guy wanted to get something done outside the normal operating channels. Corleone was both respected and feared, yet few were able to get an audience with him. Those who were fortunate enough to meet with the Godfather and ask for his help knew that he might call on them in the future for an undeniable request of his own. There was an unspoken, but expected, quid pro quo – otherwise, the consequences could be severe or even deadly. Corleone would make them an offer they couldn't refuse.

We can learn much from exploring some of the discernable characteristics of a "godfather" persona as exhibited by Marlon Brando's character in the film based on Mario Puzo's best-selling novel. A "godfather":

Has relatively humble beginnings with wealth acquired over time through shrewd business maneuvers and acquisitions;

Is strong, a survivor, unapologetic, problem solver;

Is mature, has paid his dues;

Offers unambiguous propositions, holds cards close to his vest;

Has a long memory, doesn't forget slights from his enemies or favors from his friends;

Is loyal, expects and engenders reciprocal loyalty among his family and subordinates;

Is not flashy, is understated, unsuspecting, and operates in a stealth-like fashion, often behind the scenes;

The Change[8]

Is reliable with a high level of integrity—if he says he is going to do something, he means it;

Possesses powerful friends; and

Is full of contradictions, simultaneously ruthless and loving.

Entrepreneurs are certainly not crime bosses and do not usually operate using Vito Corleone-like tactics. Yet, the position of being the person who has the connections to get things done and won't take "no" for an answer is a powerful one indeed. This individual will sometimes go it alone or sometimes work in conjunction with others. He or she has sufficient financial resources to launch a product line, build a brand, or champion an important social or political cause.

Former New York City Mayor Michael Bloomberg fits the bill as a contemporary godfather in corporate industry. An entrepreneur and philanthropist who served three terms as Mayor of New York City and is often touted as a possible presidential candidate, Bloomberg got his first job working as a parking lot attendant while attending Johns Hopkins University. He started his professional career in an entry-level job at the Wall Street firm Salomon Brothers, and quickly rose through the ranks.

Bloomberg was let go when Salomon Brothers was acquired by a larger firm in the early 1980s. He then launched a small startup business in a one-room office. Today, <u>Bloomberg LP</u> is a global financial and media conglomerate that has more than 15,000 employees and offices in 73 countries around the world. Bloomberg's personal wealth is considerable. With an estimated net worth of $33 billion, he is the <u>eleventh richest</u> person in the United States and the sixteenth wealthiest in the world.

While serving as New York's mayor, Bloomberg used his influence and strong personality to impose changes to the city which spurred economic growth and job creation. But he also used his considerable prowess to extend his time in office to an additional four years by championing a change in the city's term limit law. His pet projects include banning smoking in all indoor workplaces, as well as at parks and beaches; climate change; gun control; and immigration reform. He wields considerable political power, having been one of the largest contributors to Democratic political campaigns in the last election cycle.

Clive Davis, Grammy Award-winning record producer and music industry executive, is an example of a godfather in the entertainment industry. Davis' grooming and seal of approval have catapulted a diverse roster of talented artists to stardom, including the Jennifer Hudson, Aerosmith, Christina Aguilera, Alicia Keys, Barry Manilow, Earth, Wind & Fire, and the late Whitney Houston.

Orphaned as a teenager when both of his parents died prematurely, Davis attended college and law school on full scholarship. His professional career began as an attorney for a small New York law firm, and a few years later he was appointed as general manager of Columbia Records Group in 1965.

Davis founded Bad Boy Records with Sean "Puffy" Combs and it became the home of artists Notorious B.I.G., Mase, 112, and Faith Evans. He started J Records, an independent label in 2000, and through mergers and acquisitions, the company became part of BMG and Sony Music Entertainment. His music industry career has spanned five decades with stints at CBS Records and Arista Records.

Recording artists realize Davis' Midas touch when it comes to selecting and grooming artists who eventually become megastars. His stamp of approval and connections are often all that are needed to open all of the necessary doors that lead to an aspiring artist realizing his or her dreams of stardom and material wealth.

But you don't have to be Bloomberg or Davis to be a major player in your sphere of influence. You can be a godfather (or a godmother, for the female entrepreneurs) within your own niche by being the proverbial big fish in a little pond. In other words, you can be the most influential player within your industry, especially if you operate within a niche that is relatively small.

Position #2: The Detective (The Investigative Factor)

In contrast to the "godfather" power position, the "detective" tends to operate with an emphasis on altruism. Although extremely successful as entrepreneurs, the primary focus of the business of "detectives" involves seeking opportunities to assist or be of service to others. They are often a conduit for matching those in need with service providers, health professionals, and others who can help them solve their problems or enhance their lives.

In this age of the Internet and social media, there is no reason or excuse for someone seeking to fulfill the role of "detective" to fail to reach his/her objective. The networks you have developed on Facebook, Twitter, LinkedIn, Instagram and other social media sources give you the two key elements for solidifying your power position as a detective: 1) The ability to make others aware of your credentials, achievements, and services; and 2) The ability to identify those in your network who may have needs that you, or a business associate, can fulfill.

Via your social media network and utilizing Google searches, you can also discover potential clients' current projects and causes that they hold dear. Then you can utilize your gifts and skills to bring their goals or dreams to reality.

One of the world's more successful business "detectives" is Oprah Winfrey. Oprah has been ranked as the richest African-American of the 20th century, the greatest black philanthropist in American history, and is currently North America's only black billionaire, with an estimated net worth of $2.9 billion.

The fact that Oprah was born into poverty was likely a strong influence on her approach to her business as a talk show host and media proprietor. Born to a teenage single mother in rural Mississippi and the victim of rape at age nine, Oprah has always exhibited genuine empathy for those with limited resources or who have been persecuted, exploited, or abused. She is credited with creating a more intimate confessional form of media communication, and has launched the successful careers of dozens of physicians, attorneys, entertainers, and others, including Dr. Phil, Dr. Oz, and Rachael Ray.

During episodes of her daytime talk show, which aired for 25 years, Oprah often gave valuable gifts to members of the studio audience, including new cars, homes, trips to foreign countries, and beauty and wardrobe makeovers. She seemed to be energized by the excitement and gratitude of the recipients.

The power of Oprah's opinions and endorsements to influence public opinion, especially consumer purchasing choices, has been dubbed "The Oprah Effect." The book club she launched in 1996, for example, resulted in instant best-seller status for the authors who were lucky enough to be selected. Being recognized by Oprah often means a million additional book sales for an author, and has a positive monetary impact on all participants in the book industry distribution chain, including retailers, distributors, and publishers.

Oprah's endorsement of presidential candidate Barack Obama in the 2008 Democratic primary is believed by many to have made the difference in votes that led the Illinois Senator to victory over

Hillary Clinton. That election was the first time Oprah had ever endorsed a presidential candidate.

Through her private charity, The Oprah Winfrey Foundation, she has awarded hundreds of grants to organizations that support the education and empowerment of women, children, and families in the United States and around the world. She has donated millions of dollars toward providing a better education for students who have merit, but no means. In January 2007, she opened the Oprah Winfrey Leadership Academy for Girls in South Africa, which she hopes will develop the country's future women leaders.

The realization that you lack the vast resources that Oprah possesses should not deter you from enhancing the lives of those in your sphere of influence by being a "detective." Small acts of kindness directed toward others can have a substantial impact, and set you apart from the pack of competitors in your field.

Position #3: "The Play Maker" (The Assist Factor)

If you know anything about professional basketball, then you know that Ervin "Magic" Johnson was among the best all-around players in history. During his tenure as a college athlete as well as in the NBA, Johnson was known for being an unselfish, team player, and holds the NBA career record for highest assists per game average with 11.2. The vast majority of the time when Johnson passed the ball to a teammate, he put them in a position to score. He understood the concept that when the team won, he won too. Johnson consistently subjugated any need he may have had for personal notoriety for the team's well-being.

Upon initial examination, the status of "play maker" might seem to be disadvantageous, since it appears that others benefit more from your work than you do. Yet, many professionals have achieved tremendous success being a play maker as opposed to the celebrity.

Political consultants David Plouffe and David Axelrod, who shepherded then U.S. Senator Barack Obama's fledgling presidential campaign to victory, worked almost entirely behind the scenes, especially in the early stages of strategic planning. Few people actually expected Obama to secure the Democratic nomination, let alone be elected the nation's 43rd president. But Plouffe and Axelrod understood their roles as strategists and let Obama, the candidate, be the star attraction.

Plouffe, Axelrod, and others on the Obama planning team pored over the rules of the Democratic presidential nomination process and discovered a wrinkle in the rules that they could exploit; one they were sure that primary opponent Hillary Clinton's team would overlook: Winning the process hinged on amassing the most delegates, rather than the most overall cumulative votes. In traditionally Republican states that Clinton was likely to ignore because of the small number of Democratic voters, if Obama were to win a majority of the delegates, he could stockpile enough delegates to make up for shortfalls he might experience in larger states. Plouffe and Axelrod's strategy worked and the rest is history.

Another example of the role of professional "play maker" is an agent. Agents in the fields of sports, entertainment, and publishing operate from positions of power as virtually no deals are cut without them being involved. An agent will typically receive 3 to 15 percent of their clients' earnings for the duration of their contracts, depending on the industry. If an agent has a roster of several successful clients, he or she can rake in millions of dollars year after year, even though the deals only need to be negotiated or re-negotiated a few times.

The role of "play maker" should be viewed as an enviable position, rather than one with few rewards. This role allows you to operate under the radar, away from much of the scrutiny and opposition experienced by those who are in the limelight.

Position #4: "The Investor" (The Universal Return on Investment Factor)

The law of investment simply means that you multiply your financial resources. This is usually done by taking some of your funds or other liquid assets and putting them in a business venture or financial instrument that increases in value over a specified period of time. Those who invest their money wisely can often live entirely on the interest accrued on their investments, while the principal itself remains untouched. But you can also make an investment in someone else's life—encouragement, a referral, or advice—that reaps subsequent dividends.

One does not have to start out as a wealthy individual to be an "investor." In the perennial best-selling book _The Millionaire Next Door_, authors Thomas J. Stanley and William D. Danko explain that the typical American millionaire spends much less than he or she earns and is committed to saving a significant portion of his/her income over a long period of time.

Many wealthy individuals who have been successful investors are unassuming; they do not have the external trappings one normally associates with wealth. Rather than spend their money on "bling" – flashy jewelry, high-end cars and designer clothes – these investors keep their money in the bank, their assets are liquid, and they have real estate holdings that continually increase in value.

Billionaire Warren Buffett is probably the world's best known investor, and is one of the wealthiest businessmen and investors alive today. With a net worth of more than $50 billion, he is the second wealthiest American and the fourth wealthiest person in the world. But he is famous for his frugal lifestyle and modest appearance. As the CEO of Berkshire Hathaway, he earns a base salary of only $100,000 a year, and his salary has remained the same for the last 25 years. Most billionaires live in mansions, yet Buffett still lives in Omaha, Nebraska in the five-bedroom house he bought for $31,500 more than 50 years ago.

Buffett's success as CEO of Berkshire Hathaway has inspired investors around the world to follow his every business move. His money-making strategy is simple: "The first rule of investing is 'don't lose money,'" he said. "The second rule is 'don't forget Rule No. 1.'" He also exercises caution with an eye for detail in every business deal, and his philanthropy is known worldwide, with contributions of over $30 billion to charitable causes through the Bill and Melinda Gates Foundation.

Of course, there is only one Warren Buffett, but you, too, can adopt his successful investment techniques. Identifying people, projects, and companies where an investment will reap short-term and/or long-term financial rewards is the power move you can make to position yourself as an "investor."

Position #5: "The Believer" (The Receiver Factor)

Belief may appear to be a simple thing, but becoming a "believer" is actually the most challenging and important power position of all. Belief is infectious; if you believe in yourself, your product, or your business, others will be attracted to you and resources will flow your way. Conversely, self-doubt and disbelief are attitudes that repel financial resources. When you doubt yourself, hardly anything seems to go right. Your ability to obtain a Universal Return on Investment, or UROI, is directly related to your capacity to believe and receive.

Biblical scriptures in Malachi 3:10 tell us that, with tithing or investing in spiritual matters, God will pour out "so much blessing that there will not be room enough to store it." Our belief in our entrepreneurial endeavors works in a similar fashion. Our confidence in the success of our investments and other endeavors will reap abundant returns. The question is: What is your capacity to believe and receive? How much prosperity or abundance can you mentally accept?

Here is a visual example. A glass, water pitcher, bucket, pond, river, and ocean are all vessels which contain water. But a glass holds only a few ounces, while an ocean contains more water than can be measured. Each container can receive and hold water, but the volume of water varies from small to enormous.

The containers represent your mental capacity to believe and receive and the water symbolizes the actual blessings. The blessings may be in the form of wisdom, knowledge, opportunities, favor, prosperity, abundance, etc.

Daymond John, founder of FUBU, is an example of someone who believed and received. As a native of Queens, N.Y., in the early 1990s, John recognized an untapped market in urban apparel, one that had been neglected by other clothing companies. His first foray into the apparel market began when he wanted a tie-top hat he had seen in a popular music video, but could not find one for an affordable price. With the sewing skills he had learned from his mother, John started making the hats for himself and his friends. He sold a batch of the hats on the streets of Queens one day, and made $800 in just a few hours. At that point, all of his resources could fit in the symbolic water pitcher described above.

John's early success generated buzz about his products, and his company, FUBU, was born. With the creation of a distinctive logo that he sewed on hockey jerseys, sweatshirts, and t-shirts, John was later able to convince hip-hop superstar LL Cool J to wear FUBU clothing for a promotional campaign. This was the catalyst behind the entire hip-hop community supporting the new brand and giving it instant credibility.

Twenty years later, the capacity of John's financial resources now can fill a metaphorical ocean. Presently, as a member of the cast of ABC's entrepreneurial business show *Shark Tank*, John can help budding entrepreneurs, who have often invested their life savings to make their dream of a business concept come to fruition, realize their dreams by investing in their business deals. He can help others who believe in their dreams to receive their ultimate rewards.

Conclusion

Whether you occupy the power position of "godfather," "detective," "play maker," "investor," or "believer" will depend on your personal goals and talents. Our company can assist you with identifying the best power position for you and developing the tools to solidify your position for the long haul.

Most businesses today rely on traditional sales and marketing techniques that simply no longer work in the current environment. These conventional methods automatically put the entrepreneur in a "begging" posture that focuses on "pushing" prospective clients to buy their products or services.

A much better approach is to "pull" potential clients toward you through the magnetic attraction of your power position. Building a relationship using magnetism as the primary vehicle automatically places you in the power position and leaves a lasting, indelible impression on all within your circle of influence.

To Contact Johnny:

www.pointofconnections.com

www.facebook.com/johnny.morney

Skype: johnny.morney

Mike Greenly

Mike Greenly is a former Fortune 500 Marketing & Communications VP, now a highly effective business writer and speech coach.

Having been a corporate officer himself, Mike is comfortable dealing with executives at all levels. He is known for his ability to write and coach excellent speeches for others… capturing their thoughts and messages with clarity and creativity, while minimizing demands on their time. Clients across many industries highly praise the quality of his work, along with his unwavering commitment to outstanding client service.

Immediately after leaving corporate life, Mike became the world's first "interactive electronic journalist" … covering computer and other trade shows online, including the launch of Macintosh. He was the first journalist to report on the Democratic and Republican conventions and the Hollywood Oscars via computer. His award-winning journalism was covered by *TIME* (Nov. 25, 1985), *The Wall Street Journal*, CNN, NBC, and international media. He has consulted for the U.S.I.A. and the government of Spain.

When not writing speeches, Mike enjoys writing song lyrics. Four of his songs have been charted on Billboard. He is also the author of "Our Great Virginia" which became the state's official traditional anthem on July 1, 2015.

From "Stage Fright" to the Power of Authenticity

By Mike Greenly

In the spirit of this book – "dedicated to all those seeking change" – I'll share the story of my journey and the difference it made to my professional success and personal happiness. These days, I use the insights I've gained to help me write effective speeches for others and/or to coach them – from CEOs to Fathers of the Bride – on how to achieve greater comfort, confidence and impact with an audience.

So how do you, yourself, feel about standing on a stage, looking out at a crowd and delivering your thoughts to everyone staring back? For the first decades of my life, that was impossible for me, without feeling sick to my stomach.

There is a name for the dread of public speaking: "glossophobia." I've known for decades about surveys showing that many people fear an audience more than other phobias … like the fear of heights, darkness, death, or in my case, the dentist's drill.

Having had extreme "stage fright" for years, I changed in a big way after some transformational experiences. Not only did I learn to hold the attention of an audience—even one as large as 5,000 people— also, to my surprise, I actually learned to enjoy it!

The single most important lesson I've learned – and I'll tell you how I learned it – is to harness the power of one's own authenticity when delivering a speech or presentation. That lesson, in itself, has made a tremendous difference for me and for many others I have worked with.

I didn't start out with that understanding, however. I grew up in Beaufort, SC – on a small, beautiful island by the Atlantic. But I had the challenge of being "different."

Early on, I became aware that, in our mostly Baptist town, many people around me – children included – looked down on me for being Jewish, set apart from most others. What's more, I had skipped a grade – leaving the second for the third grade only one month into the school year. So I was younger than all my classmates.

I was also a major geek with zero athletic talent or training. During recess each day, with no friends to talk to or play with, I hid in embarrassment behind the oleander bushes against the Beaufort Elementary School walls.

Would you expect that such a boy would grow up and be able, some day, to hold an audience of 5,000 comfortably in his hands? Young Michael S. Greenly never would have guessed!

Years later, however – after Duke University and a move to New York City – I was achieving success in corporate life. I had become Assistant Publisher at Scholastic, Inc., the educational publisher. Then a promotional copywriter, and eventually a brand manager, at Lever Brothers.

With the help of the expert training I was fortunate to receive, I acquired a range of "techniques" for effective presentations. A few among them …

MOVEMENT ON-STAGE

I learned never to be one of those speakers who "wander," tracing a restless path as they talk.

If you don't know this yet, I promise that you will be more effective and convincing if you plant yourself on-stage like a steadfast pillar of authority, the Tree of Knowledge ... moving across stage only when there's an important new point to be made, or a change in mood, and then re-planting yourself.

It doesn't matter if this feels artificial to you at first. After all, you're "acting"—giving a "performance." That's not being real ... just making it feel that way. I'll say more about this in a bit.

HAND GESTURES

The best advice is the simplest: give yourself permission to be you. If you talk with your hands naturally, then do! If you don't use your hands in "real life," don't try to fake it on-stage.

Audiences crave a connection with anyone addressing them. Otherwise, you become just part of a "show"—including your gestures—without having created real engagement from your listeners.

The most important guidance is to let your mind and voice be in sync with your words. If you feel—not just think, but feel—the meaning of your words when you say them ... your audience will feel that, too. They'll sense and believe in your genuineness as you experience it, yourself.

So in whatever way your hands move (or don't) when you're expressing your own message ... that's how your hands should be on-stage.

"How do I move on-stage?" and "What do I do with my hands?" are two of the most frequent questions I encounter when I'm coaching someone new.

Having learned "basics" like these, I began giving reasonably effective presentations to my colleagues and to the staffs of the departments I ran. Secretly, however, I never felt at home with the experience of giving a speech. I remained a victim of glossophobia.

Until ... the major "aha" changed my life.

That occurred years later, after I followed a friend who had left Lever for Avon Products, Inc., a much more people-oriented company than Lever (which taught me a lot about marketing, but felt like a military bunker.) In a way, it was strange for someone like me – secretly shy and insecure – to join a company filled with so many apparent extroverts at Avon.

Avon's business model was famous for an emphasis on motivation that inspired its vast network of independent sales reps to service their customers, even on the hottest, coldest, or most difficult of days. I found myself thriving under leaders who were quick to acknowledge how hard and how intensely I strove to be excellent.

A few years later, I was put in charge of approving every aspect of 300 new products a year – each individual concept, trademarked name, product formulation, package design, promotional positioning and so on. Later, I ran the merchandising department, responsible for the profit and loss of the entire U.S. product line and its biweekly sales campaigns.

The exposure was remarkable – from leading a class on direct selling communications in Tokyo, to giving a speech in French to sales managers in Marseilles. All the while, however, I suffered my

The Change[8]

private "stage fright" before every presentation. Until my "aha" moment.

That came only after I was promoted to Vice President of Field Support, with all communications for the U.S. sales force under my purview. Once again, I was "the youngest" – in this case, they said, the youngest VP in the history of this century-old company.

I was whisked up to the executive floor and given a lavish budget to redecorate the office to my taste – one of the perks of being an Avon VP. Every inch of my surroundings – carpeting, couch, desk, guest chairs – was designed to my specifications: an astonishing luxury for a kid from a tiny island down South.

But old insecurities haunted me still. They were amplified by the presence of an established VP down the hall who soon began to feel like a rival … a competitor in what was supposed to be a united team of Officers Together.

I'll call him Big Guy, since if he wasn't precisely 6'8", he was nonetheless an unusually tall and towering man with a huge and overwhelming personality. He was the extrovert's extrovert, fearless in displaying his (undeniable) creativity and charisma.

At that point, he was in charge of creating the Avon sales brochure – 22 million magazines published every two weeks, filled with money-making ads with "specials" on products, available only during that "campaign." My role was to motivate the field to use his selling tools to produce the greatest possible revenue.

Part of my new assignment was to be in charge of the August Conference – the annual sales meeting for District Sales Managers from around the country. By the time they headed back home, they were to be pumped up with enthusiasm and "belief," ready to ignite passion within the hundreds of reps they managed locally.

Not only was I responsible for producing the meeting to achieve that result, but as the VP in charge, I also was required to give a speech of my own ... from the same stage where I'd observed and been in awe of Big Guy delivering his booming, Carnival Barker performances in full strut.

The familiar dread of public speaking came back to haunt me, as I started planning the Conference and my remarks. What a timid little mouse I would surely seem like, in contrast to Big Guy. The more I realized that I could never be like him – that I would fail if I tried – the more miserable I became.

Until ... it clicked in my brain that, instead of trying to be a pale imagination of Big Guy, what I actually needed to be was the best version of myself.

Off-stage, I am his opposite in many ways. It's simply not within me to bully or badger someone to achieve my goals, nor to be strident or flamboyant. One friend named me years ago, "the most earnest person on the Eastern Seaboard" – intensely sincere, but much too polite and empathetic to overwhelm others, even as a negotiating technique.

Of course, my on-stage rival's style worked beautifully for him. I had witnessed for years how brilliantly dynamic he was on-stage. But as with shoes that won't fit, I suddenly understood that his way of presenting would be awkward and uncomfortable for me.

That fundamental idea – being true to myself instead of straining to be a pale imitation of someone else – is stupidly simple and obvious to me now. But what a difference it made when I applied it!

When the time came for my motivational message—my turn to inspire—I didn't try to be flashy like my colleague. Instead, I addressed the audience in a simple and personal way. I recalled my

The Change[8]

first week with the company – when they sent me to Iowa to see what "direct selling" was really like.

Here is the story I told …

You know enough about me now, and my shy and lonely childhood, to imagine how mortifying it had been for me, on my first day in the field – to knock on strangers' doors for "cold-call" selling. I did my best to simulate a cheerful "Avon Calling!" greeting … at least to those who were home. But it was an excruciating day. I got a firsthand sense of how difficult and intimidating life could be for a new Avon rep.

Only one customer actually bought from me – a single bottle of nail polish. I was grateful for the sale, as pitifully small as it was.

As I reminisced about that experience in my speech to the District Manager audience, I recalled how amazing it had been – the next day in Iowa – to travel around with the best sales rep in the region. Her selling effectiveness was completely different from mine. Her customers welcomed her as they would a delightful friend. They trusted her, depended on her and – it was clear – they truly liked her.

After our day together … after I'd seen how remarkably successful Avon's distribution channel could be … this outstanding rep praised her Manager for the training and encouragement that had led to what I witnessed. Now that she brought home more income than her factory-worker husband, she said, he viewed her with new respect and appreciation. This enthusiastic "Avon Lady" had become his equal in the family.

Just as meaningful to her was the way her children now looked up to her. (Remember, this was decades ago.) She took enormous pleasure in their awareness that Mom was a much more powerful and capable figure than they had imagined.

But the most pivotal change in her life, she said – as her comments moved and excited me about the company I'd just joined – was the self-esteem she had gained. She directly attributed her newfound pride and happiness to her supportive Manager.

While sharing this story on-stage with my sales management audience, I did not gallivant across the space trying to simulate the extroverted "showman" I'll never be. Instead, I consciously allowed myself to get back in touch with the real emotion I had felt in discovering how my new company had enhanced an Iowa housewife's life ... thanks to the training and guidance of her Manager.

As I recalled and re-experienced those feelings under the spotlight, while praising my sales management audience for the daily impact that had on the lives of those they led ... I heard sniffles and occasional sobs from around the giant hotel ballroom. I knew beyond doubt that I was having a significant impact on my audience, simply by being "me" ... sincere, earnest, and emotional.

Afterward, countless attendees came up to grasp my hands or give me hugs. Over and over they said: "one of the best speeches ever!" That crucial lesson, about the power of being true to one's essence, has been incredibly useful ever since, both on- and off-stage.

When I write speeches for executives these days, that insight helps me live up to the slogan I developed for my Internet ads: "Sound like yourself ... only better." And when I coach executives – many of whom are secretly as nervous as I used to be – I draw on my story to help them find new poise and security as they speak.

Yes, there are "techniques" and "tricks" for being effective on-stage: how to stand, when to move, what to with your hands, how to modulate your voice, etc. These even involve details like how to turn from one page of your script to the next, if you're standing at a podium and working from a paper copy. Or how to use a TelePrompter, so that you – not the machine's operator – remain confidently and smoothly in control.

One imperative I've learned, which many presenters underestimate, is the importance of the right kind of rehearsal ... both quantity and quality.

QUANTITY:

You want to rehearse your text so often that you know the material well enough to be comfortable and un-strained, looking up from the page and finishing a sentence before looking down for the next cue.

This is not the same as "memorizing" a word-for-word script, even though many regulated industries require lawyer-vetted scripting. Having to rely solely on memory puts tremendous pressure on a speaker and requires a greater investment in time and technique for natural, relaxed delivery.

QUALITY:

The way you rehearse can make a surprising difference during your ultimate presentation.

Of much greater consequence than the number of times you rehearse is how you do it. The more mentally "real" you can make each run-through, the more confident and effective you'll be in front of your audience.

Forget forever about reviewing the words of your speech in silence. NO! That misses the point. Making rehearsal real means actively envisioning everyone in front of you – every time you rehearse – and always addressing them aloud, with the same energy you expect to use on-stage.

Again: rehearse aloud, including imaginary eye contact with your pretend audience. (Good quality rehearsal is fatiguing – like a real presentation.)

The right kind of rehearsal also means being as conscious of your pacing and variety as you would want to be in front of in-person listeners ... every single time you rehearse. Making each rehearsal as much like "the real thing" as you can will pay off in your eventual delivery.

The paradox of being effective in delivering a speech is learning to be authentic on the one hand ... while always remembering that a speech is also a "performance." It's both real and artificial, at once.

It takes focus, energy, and the right kind of rehearsal to effectively project yourself as you speak. Many speakers write notes to themselves in their texts: reminders during delivery to SMILE ... show ENERGY ... be FRIENDLY, etc.

One needs to be a "bigger" version of one's self in front of hundreds of people or more. It will not work to address an audience in the same way you might chat with a friend over coffee. The physical gap between you and your audience is psychological, too. Your audience will not be aware of it, but it affects their ability to maximally "connect" with you.

The literal gap is about height (you're standing, they're sitting) and distance (between the front row and where you stand.) To overcome it requires most presenters to be more energized, with more presence, than they ever would be off-stage.

You want each member of the audience to feel as though you're talking to and connecting directly and personally ... and to feel as though you're not as far away as, in fact, you are.

It can require a change of one's mindset to be one's own authentic self – while, paradoxically, also being better and bigger on-stage. But the core truth in everything I use in coaching my clients is the one that changed me and my life: drawing on and making the most of the inherent power of who I am ... never trying to be an imitation of someone else, no matter how effective that other person might appear to be.

So when you're faced with the challenge of giving a speech ... no matter how tense or fretful you feel ... take stock of who you are. For real. Connect to the truth at the heart of your personal brand. Be in touch with your genuine essence as you speak.

As I've mentioned, there are a number of "tips" that can help one be more effective. But the single most important technique is that simple, but essential mindset – finding the courage to be your own real self on-stage (only "bigger").

I can tell you this with certainty: it is possible to make that change. And it's very satisfying when you do. It can make all the difference in enabling you to hear one of the sweetest sounds on earth: the applause that you have earned for who you actually are.

Mike Greenly

Website: www.mikegreenly.com/

Phone: 212-758-5338

Email: greenlypro@mikegreenly.com

Facebook: www.facebook.com/mikegreenly

Twitter: www.twitter.com/MikeGreenly

LinkedIn: www.linkedin.com/in/WriterCoachMikeGreenly

Mache Torres

She recently married her long-time fiancé', David Ackerman, and now is a mother of five beautiful girls.

Graduated from De La Salle University with a Marketing Management Degree & Master's Degree in Educational Leadership and Management.

Took advanced courses in Medical Hypnotherapy-

A 5th Path Hypnotherapist and a 7th Path Self-Hypnosis teacher, graduated from the Banyan Institute of Hypnosis in Orange County, California.

As an educator, she is a co-owner and a Board of Trustee of the family-owned school business, St. James College System, in the Philippines.

As a philanthropist and a civic leader with a big heart, she founded TASA -Transformational Advocacy Thru Self Awareness and a Charter President of the Rotary Club of Makati Business District.

Founder/ CEO of Mache Torres Advocacy & Leadership Programs, Inc.

As a life coach who empowers and inspires, she specializes in traumas; childhood issues; emotional instability; self-leadership/awareness; relationships/marital problems; addiction and depression.

She is an author of the books *Passionately with No Bounds!* And *You Are Brand New!*, which will be launched soon.

So Near Yet So Far

By Mache Torres

The hardest person to reach is the one nearest us ... the SELF. We have the tendency to wear blinders and see only what is in front of us. In times of crises, we simply look far ahead for solutions.

This reminds me of the song, "I've Never Been To Me." This is a song about a woman who has been to many places around the world and has done a lot of things that she thinks is the best in her life. She thinks that she has been to "paradise," yet she has not been to herself. As a stanza goes, "I've been to paradise, but I've never been to me." After all, she does not feel fulfilled and wished that she had a talk with herself. She then realizes that she does not really know her real self!

Traveling and seeing the world is a great escape. It is a great way of discovering new things, new experiences, and new cultures. For some, this is a once-in-a-lifetime experience – great for couples or for family bonding. For others, traveling is an escape to forget problems or personal issues. After all, traveling can always be fun and enjoyable. But one should always learn from it...

It can even be a chance for introspection ... through retrospection.

Introspection is when one looks into his or her feelings and emotions. Retrospection is when one looks into his/her past. Both processes are important because they help a person focus on what can be controlled, which are internal issues. Some people tend to focus on external issues which are beyond their control. In effect, it causes unnecessary stress.

However, it is not that easy for some people to go through introspection or retrospection.

We tend to miss out on the power of introspection because issues may come our way. These may be about the family and relationships or work and business. Then there are people who are afraid to look back and to retrospect. They would even try to forget their painful experiences.

Human nature dictates that it is always convenient to blame others rather than to look into one's self. It is a basic human trait – self-defense. But is this the best way to resolve and face the real issue at hand?

The movie *Kung Fu Panda* (2008) illustrates this. The panda wanted to be a great Kung Fu master. He had to climb the highest mountain in order to find the secret on how to be the greatest dragon warrior. He reached the mountain summit and found the treasure box that held the secret—a scroll with nothing on it but a mirror reflection. He was surprised to find out that there was really no secret but to see oneself. He had to see his own reflection to learn that the greatest strength should come from within. It was talking about the power of having inner strength.

My Journey

My personal journey started when I had to leave and take a break from my painful world due to a failed marriage.

After a seven-year marriage, I found myself in a very scary situation of possibly becoming a single mom with four wonderful daughters. Everything was crumbling around me. My kids were confused about what was going to happen next. I thought that being around my kids was the best thing for me while I went through the healing process. I didn't realize that the wound was so deep that I could not hide nor pretend to my kids that I was ok.

In effect, seeing me cry and be so devastated made them feel more uncertain of what was going to happen to our family. I tried so hard to fix what was broken. I tried so hard to make the family complete again. Then I realized that it always takes two to tango. It takes two to break a marriage and on the other hand, it takes two to fix a marriage as well.

It hurt me so much to be judged by many who could never understand my situation. I was being judged by people who lacked compassion and experience. It was also during this lowest time of my life that I learned who my real friends were. Only then did I learn to seek help from those "who had been there and done that." These people did not just have the compassion, but they could also share what they had learned from what they had been through.

Growing up as a Catholic, and coming from a Catholic school, it was embedded in my belief that no matter what, a marriage should stay intact. It was so hard for me to move on and to file for an annulment, since I was still hoping for a possible reconciliation.

Then, I talked to a priest who I vividly remember saying, "If you have done everything that is humanly possible, then it is the time to let go and to let God … You deserve to be happy and to focus on yourself. You are not doing this just for yourself, but for your children as well because they will be happy if they see you happy." After having heard that, I felt the energy of the divine Holy Spirit come unto me.

This was the start of my awakening, realizing that the "self" has been suffering from too much anger, confusion, fear, and anxiety. These were powerful negative emotions that stopped me from seeing the

The Change[8]

bigger picture. My self-esteem was just so low that I blamed everything on myself. I was filled with guilt that I could not be the best for my children during those darkest moments in my life.

Our culture has impacted my personal acceptance, having believed that a woman should always take a back seat, should always take the blows, and should accept all the lies, just for the sake of saving the family. Until then, I realized that everything happened because I let it happen. Did I want my own children, who are all girls, to experience the same thing? Did I want them to believe that they are only second class because they are women? Did I want them to allow men to treat them badly because they are made to feel that they are never good enough? Of course not!

Due to the old school teachings, children before were always taught not to interject opinions while the grown-ups were talking. We were not supposed to be seen or heard during adult conversations. This practice has inhibited self-expression.

Having seen the negative effects of this, I learned how to listen and let my children express themselves. After all, "All feelings are good"—we just need to learn how to validate our emotions to understand the inner struggles.

I am glad that my girls learned and are learning from what I have been thru. I want them to understand and to believe that they are all precious and nobody can make them feel otherwise. I want them to realize that being a woman is not a liability. I want them to learn that women in society are meant to inspire and are big contributors to the community. I want them to feel that they deserve to be respected as they respect themselves. It is for them to learn that they cannot live in lies… the truth should always prevail.

After all those years of retrospection, I realized that what did happen was meant to happen. It was not easy to accept that my marriage was too damaged and could no longer be salvaged. Acceptance was obviously always the first step to healing...

My Healing

How can a mother be at her best for her children if she herself is so unhappy and uncertain?

I barely recognized myself. My ability to look at the bigger picture became impaired due to overwhelming negative emotions. My world became smaller, as I had to detach myself from the judgment of society.

I was just so lucky to have very supportive parents and siblings who gave me the chance to leave, to take a break, and to take care of myself. I was very certain that my girls would be left in better hands during that dark moment of my life.

I had to take a break from family, work, and friends. How could one lead others without leading oneself? I made sure that the trips I had away from my kids were productive.

Meeting the right people along my path was necessary. I had to trust my Higher Power that He would guide me to the perfect situation, and the perfect people. I focused on self-healing, self-discovery, and self-empowerment.

One can never control others but, he/she can control himself/herself. Some of us have the tendency to do things out of distraction—this is the part when one refuses to introspect ...

So the focus was within me. I thought that I knew myself well, until I realized all those negative emotions had simply buried the real me.

Forgiveness has been a key word to moving forward. Easy to say, hard to do. And how???

The Change[8]

I have attended several group sessions on healing and forgiveness. However, hearing other people's personal testimonies confused me.

I thought that these sessions aimed at having the participants thank the people who have hurt them, knowing that they needed forgiveness and gratitude to learn their real purpose, and thereby realize that one's purpose had to come from one's own learning. But this was not so.

The people in the group sessions would relate their experiences, and they would express these with so much emotion, full of pain and anger. Yet, they said that they had forgiven those who had hurt them. Based on my personal experience, I would define real forgiveness as being when one can relate his/her story with so much passion to inspire, and with acknowledgement to thank the people who have hurt them. I call it "tears of gratitude"!

I am expressing my personal gratitude to those who have hurt me, as I would not be here without going through the journey of self-discovery. My forgiveness was based on who I became after extracting the learning from my experiences.

My deepest gratitude goes as well to my personal friend and mentor who has taught me to go back to the basics of prayers. Aside from focusing on my inner self, I would not have made it without my trust and faith in God, my Higher Power.

Through perfect faith and prayers, I was able to find the hope that I needed to start over. I then rediscovered the concealed greatness within me. I found my core where my inner child is hidden due to all the negative emotions that hindered my personal growth. I had to befriend the "Little Mache," the little child that I once were—the loved, loving, and lovable little me, who was longing for my reconnection and attention.

Embracing My Purpose

The search of my purpose in life was so strong that I knew I had to move on to a much greater calling...

My travels abroad (i.e., Singapore, different cities in the US) became beneficial since my focus was self-discovery and healing. My main internal struggle was: "What is my real purpose in life? Why am I going through all this? Why me?"

These questions gave way to deeper introspection through retrospection. After reviewing all the past hurts, anger, and fears, I realized that I could never move on without unloading these emotional burdens that held me from moving on.

Having learned self-hypnosis from a Singaporean-based Peruvian hypnotherapist, who now is my dear friend, I knew that everything had to happen for a purpose ... This skill has helped me to unload all the past hurts easily, forgive unconditionally, focus on the now, and to program the future.

After unloading all the pain of the past, I had a clearer vision of my path—the path that had been there the whole time, but was not taken. The answers that I had been longing for were just in front of my face. The people that needed to be appreciated were just there, waiting for my readiness. My visions of my commitment and calling to help other families, women, and children were clearer.

My journey will not stop here. This is not just about how it helped me move on and grow. My journey continues, as I had to learn the skills to help others as well. Through my Peruvian mentor, I met her American mentor who trained her and others to be the top 1% of hypnotherapists. In one of my trips to the United States, I was led to meet him again for a greater purpose. And that was when I decided to become one of them.

Empowering Others

As a life coach, working with single women/men and single mothers was truly fulfilling.

The common issue is why they cannot find a good man or woman? This again emanates from the similar issue of not learning from the past relationship/s. Looking too far than seeing the self. A person radiates the kind of energy that he or she possesses. Self-awareness is very important before one can establish relationships. This doesn't just apply to romantic relationships, but even with family, friends, at work, and in society.

Unfortunately, women who have low self-esteem often unconsciously exude a "victim" aura. So the men that they attract are the men who easily prey on women who are vulnerable and impressionable. Based on studies, the human nature of men in general is to conquer and they are afraid of commitment until they find the right one.

Attracting the right man/woman will depend on the readiness of the person. Especially for women, one needs to establish the self-respect and inner-strength to possess the energy of an empowered woman, a woman who knows what she wants and what she truly deserves.

Some may have confusion between narcissism and self-empowerment. Narcissism is when one is just focused on the self without thinking of the effect on others; whereas self-empowerment is when you know that you have the inner strength to fight for what is fair for yourself and for others.

Some men have work-related issues. Like, how to deal with their bosses, or how to maximize their potentials for a possible promotion, or how to succeed in their businesses.

I would call some of them little boys trapped in an adult body. In retrospection, seeing their childhood, most of them realize that they are stuck due to traumas in school, like from being bullied and from being branded by their parents, such as: "you will never be good enough" or "you are too young to know these things" or "you are a loser and will never learn". And much worse, "you are a man and you are not supposed to cry." Does this mean that men are not as human as women and that they are not allowed to have feelings?

Those are mean words that came from their own parents or teachers. Sad to say, but these parents and teachers were products of the old school way of teaching. We cannot blame them because they themselves were brought up that way. They thought that it was the best way to raise a child and to push them to be better people, without realizing the effects on the child's subconscious mind.

In effect, the person lacks self-confidence at work. He thinks that he will never be good enough for a promotion or to start a business venture. After unloading the painful past, befriending the real self, and knowing one's purpose, the self can reach his/her fullest potential.

One of my personal advocacies as well is to help women inside the Correctional Institutional for Women. I reach out to these troubled women, especially those who are suffering from depression. They may have been sentenced for years or even for a lifetime of imprisonment, but they are still entitled to their right to have peace of mind – inner peace. I established regular transformational sessions with these women, which I call "Inner Peace Talks." They are given the chance to introspect through retrospection. They revisit whatever they have done in the past that caused them to be imprisoned. They are guided to learn from it so they can have self-forgiveness, which is most of the time the hardest thing to do.

Aside from this special group of women who suffer from depression, I also help the ones who are about to be freed soon. These are the ladies who have almost served their sentence and are being prepared to face the world again. I help them understand and realize that they can always start anew, even after being imprisoned. "Starting anew" means that one has learned from the past mistakes and has resolved the real root cause of the problem. This is key to avoid any repetition of the situation. Some are unconsciously repeating the situations in their lives like a vicious cycle. The unconscious reaction is a result of things embedded in the subconscious that are not realized or processed by the conscious mind.

In reaching out to the female inmates, the greatest things I learned is not to judge. It's hard to understand a person if you don't know what he or she has gone through.

Living in a country where having a therapist is taboo is so sad. Most people would rather keep personal issues within themselves, rather than be branded "crazy." There is even an increase suicides and attempted suicides due to unresolved inner conflicts. Seeking help and advice is a sign of humility and openness to change.

After all, the nearest person is not at all too far to reach. After gaining the needed inner strength, the SELF will always feel safe, secure, and loved.

To Contact Mache:

Website: www.machetorres.com

Email: machetorres412@yahoo.com

SKYPE: mache888

VIBER: 639175940412

Mary Cheyne

Mary Cheyne (pronounced 'Sheen'), MBA, was once a self-conscious public speaker and communicator. She has spent the past 13 years learning and mastering effective communication skills.

In 2009, she competed in the World Championship of Public Speaking and out of 25,000 contestants from 14 countries, she placed second.

Now, Mary is a professional speaker and trainer. As president of Magnetic Podium, LLC, her own training and communications company, she teaches people to communicate clearly both in front of an audience as well as in personal conversations at corporations and organizations. She also teaches communications-related classes at Northeastern University in Boston. Mary has trained over 15,000 people in over 25 cities around the world and has coached hundreds of individuals on how to become better speakers and communicators.

Mary's communications accolades have been featured in *The Boston Globe*, *The World Journal*, as well as many TV and radio interviews. She is also the author and creator of the audio program "Shortcut to Speaking Success."

Mary grew up in Sydney, Australia and moved to the United States in 2001. She lives in Boston with her husband and two-year-old son

Conscious Communication:

Your Prescription for Best Outcomes and Fulfilling Relationships

By Mary Cheyne

For the most part, I grew up in a "normal" family. But the way we communicated during disagreements was not ideal. As a child, I frequently witnessed my parents fighting. When an intense argument arose, I always thought there must be a better way to communicate.

As an adult, I have come to discover that dysfunctional arguments between people are common. Do you remember seeing grown-ups communicating dysfunctionally? Now we are the grown-ups.

In my own relationships, I repeated the same dysfunctional communication patterns I unknowingly absorbed. I wanted to create a better environment to raise my son in, where adults behave like adults. No more screaming matches, name-calling, or aggression. Applied globally, peace could perhaps replace war before we blow ourselves up.

That's what this chapter is about: becoming a conscious communicator to help create fulfilling relationships in your life and being able to have conversations with anyone resulting in the best outcome.

What Is Conscious Communication?

I define *conscious communication* as adopting a *conscious mindset* so our past is not in the way of the present and using a set of *concrete tools* to communicate clearly.

Why Be a Conscious Communicator?

Imagine having the mindset and concrete tools to speak with anyone that matters to you, relating in a way that is deeper and more fulfilling than your ordinary connections. Conscious communication makes that possible.

As a bonus, you're contributing to a larger cause of transforming human communications on this planet by setting an example for how conflicts can be resolved rationally, peacefully, and consciously.

I invite you to actively, fully participate in creating, living, and demonstrating a better way of communicating.

Our Innate Obstacles

Conscious communication is easier said than done. It was not taught in school. It's not our natural way of communicating. As human beings, we often sabotage our ability to communicate clearly and without judgment. Here are just a few examples.

We have filters. Specific past experiences, assumptions, and beliefs determines the color through which a person experiences the communication being received.

We want to be right. As humans with egos, we frequently like to be right, which often means making someone else wrong. While we all do it, it requires awareness to notice it.

Pay-offs for being right include:

Feeling superior or justified

The Change[8]

Avoiding taking responsibility

Going on the offense to prove you're right before someone proves you're wrong

Costs of being right include:

Loss of love and affinity

Loss of opportunity for connection

Loss of opportunity for best outcome

Ego takes over. We all have egos. The ego enjoys being superior to others and avoids the pain of looking bad, embarrassed, feeling rejected, foolish, and so on. Our egos sometimes take over when we're not paying attention.

We make meaning. As human beings, we tend to make meaning about things that happen, whether they're true or not. For example, someone gives you a sideways glance and you make the meaning they don't like you.

We defend and justify. Byron Katie, author of *Loving What Is*, says, "As soon as you defend, you're at war." In a conflict situation, defending your point of view is often like being in combat mode.

We want to fix. Humans are natural problem-solvers. Our first instinct is to fix everything, often proposing solutions when someone just needs to vent. This can make things worse.

We are distracted. In conversations, we tend not to pay full attention. We're often unfocused, preparing what we're going to say next, or thinking about lunch, or maybe even judging the person speaking.

What is the Solution?

To overcome our innate obstacles and become conscious communicators, we must look at both the mindset and the mechanics.

PART 1- The Conscious Mindset

The prerequisite of being a conscious communicator is being *mindful and aware*. Mindfulness is the container in which conscious communication takes place.

Jon Kabat-Zinn, author of *Wherever You Go, There You Are*, says, "Mindfulness is paying attention on purpose, non-judgmentally, in the present moment as if your life depended on it."

Here are some tips on being mindful:

Show Up

Showing up means bringing your entire awareness and attention to the person and the conversation. While he's talking, you're completely listening, without preparing what you're going to say next, without judgment, without an agenda. You completely hear and experience his point of view.

Choose Who Speaks

Being mindful and aware also means distinguishing your higher-self voice from your lower-self voice at any given moment. A friend asked me to borrow money multiple times. The problem is she never paid any of it back. Here was the dialogue inside my head:

Lower-Self: Why can't she be responsible for herself? She should act like an adult.

Higher-Self: You know, you can afford the amount she asked for. And in the past, she's helped me, so I should be able to help her.

Lower-Self: But what if she keeps coming back for more? Then I'm enabling her. She's clearly not borrowing money, she never pays it back.

Higher-Self: She's helped me before like when I was sick and she watched my baby. The least I could do is help her when she needs it.

The lower-self voice is not bad. A lawyer could argue a case from both sides. Here's the cool part — I get to choose which I listen to.

From a conscious place, I use one simple criterion to determine which I listen to: Which voice is more empowering and loving? The answer always inevitably is: the Higher-Self.

Be Aware of What Triggers You

When our buttons are pressed, it triggers an unpleasant emotional reaction. Gary Zukav, author of *Spiritual Partnership,* calls this phenomenon, "The frightened parts of our personality."

A big part of being mindful and conscious is to notice and catch those internal reactions before you react verbally. Get familiar with your "emotional" buttons, so when they are pressed, you're aware of what's happening and why you suddenly feel upset, angry, scared, rejected, blamed, controlled, abandoned, insulted and so on.

A situation that triggers a past emotional pain kicks off the associated chemical reactions within the body, causing that same pain to be re-experienced.

You may not even realize that a past emotional pain is playing out as though it's happening now. Eckhart Tolle, author of *The Power of Now,* calls this sensation your "pain body."

One of my trigger points is when my husband travels. Abruptly, my husband will say, "I have to fly out tomorrow." I suddenly feel abandoned, and my pain body takes over, reacting with: "You take me for granted! You don't appreciate me!" And on and on. Thirty minutes later, after the pain dissipates from my body, I realize that my past pain from childhood memories of when my mum traveled has completely hijacked my brain, and I have been in unconscious mode.

Often these emotional/body painful reactions are subtle and tricky to see. Have the intention to look for them.

Be aware of what triggers you.

Witnessing Emotional Reactions

In ninth-grade chemistry class, my teacher demonstrated a chemical reaction. She lit a strip of magnesium and it sparkled like mini fireworks. It didn't stop until the entire strip had burned down.

That's what an emotional reaction is like. An emotional reaction is also a chemical reaction, except you can't see it with your physical eyes because it's happening within your own body. But you can still witness the emotions taking place with your mind's eye. For example, "I'm noticing anger arising in me. It feels like heat and tightness in my chest. The intensity is spreading to my throat."

By being a witness as the emotional energy moves through your body, you're redirecting your focus away from your story. In my experience, your story takes you out of being mindful. For example, your story might be, "How dare he be that selfish (anger). Doesn't he have *any* feelings?"

While witnessing the emotional chemical reaction in your body, allow it to move through you. I think of "E-motion" being short for "Energy in motion." If you're in a safe place and you feel like saying something, say it. If you feel like crying, cry. If you feel like shouting, shout. You can scream into a pillow, go to the gym to work out your frustrations, or even just write in a journal. In my experience, fully feeling the emotion helps it pass through you most efficiently. Don't suppress it. Resistance blocks the energy from being released.

Allow emotion to move through you.

Widen the Gap

By being a witness to the physical sensations including any unpleasant emotions, you're widening the gap between stimulus and response. This gives you time to choose your response rather than reacting out of habit.

On a hot day my sister said to me, "Why don't you just take your son out in a diaper? You make dressing him such a big deal." I felt like she was criticizing me and felt very annoyed. In the past, I would have reacted in defense by saying, "You're being disrespectful!" Instead, I witnessed my reactions within myself. I saw my emotion of annoyance arise and then fade within my body. From there I responded with, "It's good to know that's an option."

Watching my emotional reaction gave me the little time I needed to choose my response rather than reacting out of defense.

Ego

A conscious communicator leaves his ego at the door.

PART 2- Communication Tools: The Mechanics

Once you're being mindful and aware, you've established the empty container for communicating consciously. Now you'll need a set of tools to use in conversations (the communication itself).

You use the tools outlined below to actively relate with people and to communicate clearly.

Point of View

During a course I attended, the instructor asked for two volunteers. He held a book between them. The book had a green front and a red back cover. He told the two volunteers, Sally and David, "Argue with each other: what color is the book?"

David, who was facing the front of the book said, "It's green!" Sally, who was facing the back cover, said, "It's red." This went back and forth for a while until the instructor physically positioned David next to Sally, so David said, "Oh yes, now I see the book is red."

This simple exercise was very powerful, because it illustrated that two points of view can be true at the same time.

In a conscious conversation, multiple views can be valid simultaneously. None is right or wrong. Purposefully step over to see the world from their viewpoint. Looking at why the other person sees things differently will hopefully, naturally solicit more compassion from you.

Use point of view to create common understanding.

Point of View Police

When building a common understanding and practicing seeing things from the other person's point of view, you can be your own police. In your mind, flash a blue light when you find yourself thinking, "I'm right and she's wrong." If the blue light persists, sound off a siren with a cop's voice in your head announcing, "Warning! Warning! You're straying away from point of view and saying right and wrong. Let it go. Come back to conscious awareness." Each time you drop trying to be right, your muscle for noticing it grows.

Be your own point of view police.

Re-creation

I learned this tool during a leadership course. Using this tool has paid dividends over and over again, both in my professional and personal relationships.

You use the re-creation tool to enter someone else's world. The essence of re-creating someone is to create for them what they are communicating to you. You take in what they say and then say it back to them based on your understanding.

Initially, think of it as paraphrasing. Put what they've said in your own words and say it back to them. As you become more advanced at re-creation, you can lead in with phrases like:

"What I'm hearing is…" or

"It sounds like…"

Recently, I met with a friend. Brad is a consultant at a hospital. Here's our conversation.

Me: Brad, how's your job going?

Brad: I like it. It uses my skills and I enjoy the flexibility. But I'm not sure if it's the job I want to be in forever. I'm contemplating going into real estate. But I haven't decided yet.

Me – re-creating Brad: What I'm hearing is that while you like your current job and you're pretty good at it, it doesn't quite fulfill you.

Brad (his eyes lighting up): "Yes, that's it!"

When I introduce re-creation in my workshops, I split students into pairs and have them take turns re-creating their partner. Afterwards, I ask them to reflect and share what they noticed during this exercise. Here are the most common responses:

"I realized that if I'm not listening, I can't re-create my partner."

"When my partner re-created me, I felt understood."

Re-creation lets you experience the other person's world.

Re-Creating an Angry Person

It's one thing to re-create someone who's calm and friendly. But it's another level of challenge to be mindful and conscious when someone is angry, irked, or exasperated.

I was training a group of 20 corporate employees on a new software system. I was just about to introduce myself to the class when a man in his early thirties wearing a bright purple shirt jumped up from his chair like a Jack-in-the-box and yelled, "I hate your software!"

If you were in my shoes, what would you have said? I felt my heart racing. I heard my inner dialogue say, "What am I going to do? How should I handle this?" But then my training in conscious communication and re-creation took over.

I got present to what he was saying. I listened to his words and observed his body language: He looked strained, was not smiling, and slightly rolled his eyes. I let my emotional reaction of fear rise and fade in me before I responded with:

"It sounds like you're very frustrated with the software system."

He replied, "Yes!" And I saw a look of relief on his face, as if to say, "Someone finally understands."

You can use the re-creation tool to re-create anybody, no matter how unpleasant the situation might seem.

Re-creating people makes them feel understood.

Making a Request

You can make a request of someone without letting fear of the outcome stop you. Don't avoid making requests because you're afraid of a "no." For example, my friend Alexa asked her brother, Michael, to talk with her after a spat. Michael said "no" to each of her six requests. Alexa became discouraged because she was afraid of hearing another "no." I reminded Alexa that when you make a request, the response will only be one of three outcomes:

Accept your request

Deny your request

Make you a counter offer

Each one of the three outcomes is equally valid, so don't make meaning and let fear of the outcome prevent you from initiating requests.

Making Requests Can Be Uncomfortable

On a work project with my colleague Scott, I needed him to contribute more effort. Knowing he often reacts defensively to constructive feedback, I procrastinated making the request to talk. Eventually I had to ask because the project's success was at stake. Scott was initially defensive, but he also upped his efforts in the end. What I learned is that making a request is helpful, despite being uncomfortable sometimes.

Acknowledgment

I facilitated a team-building day at an organization with the objective of highlighting areas where team effectiveness could be improved.

While interviewing individual team members to prepare for the session, one clear point stood out. A common denominator among all team members was the feeling that their efforts were not acknowledged nearly enough. Many shared that this was impacting their morale and performance.

This was an eye-opening example of how important it is to acknowledge people. Everyone seeks validation and appreciation.

You can use acknowledgment as a tool to validate people in both your professional and personal life.

Keep it simple and sincere. For example, you can say "Susan, I'd like to acknowledge you for being a quick learner."

Receiving Acknowledgment

For some people, it's also challenging to receive acknowledgment. They feel uncomfortable or even embarrassed. When someone acknowledges you, accept it graciously. For example: If someone says, "I acknowledge you for your computer skills." Resist deflecting it or playing it down like saying, "They don't call me a geek for nothing," or "Oh, it's nothing."

Instead, simply respond with, "Thank you."

It's a Process

Adopting the mindset and remembering to continuously use the tools of conscious communication takes commitment and discipline.

It takes time and consistent practice for this to become your natural way of communicating.

Committing and Recommitting

Once you've made conscious communications a priority in your life, you'll naturally gravitate towards self-policing and self-managing. If you slip up and revert to old habits, like getting triggered and reacting, it's OK. Take responsibility and then immediately recommit.

I equate being a conscious communicator to being consciously healthy. Choosing to eat in healthful ways and to exercise regularly is more than a fad. It's a lifestyle. If one night you splurge on junk food, simply return to eating healthy the next day. It's a choice in each moment, a commitment to yourself and those you love. And so is being a conscious communicator.

Conscious Communication Is a Muscle

Understand that like any new skill, conscious communication is a muscle that you build over time, a little at a time. If you wanted to lift 100 pound weights, you might begin with 10 pounds for a week then 12 pounds, and so on.

Be Patient

Using the conscious communications tools can make immediate differences in your relationships. With specific challenging relationships it may take longer; don't give up. With practice, you'll be able to have any conversation, even uncomfortable ones, more easily.

The Practice

Practice taking 100 percent responsibility for initiating conscious communication and work on releasing the emotional triggers from the past. Don't play victim by blaming other people or wishing they behaved differently. Instead, practice staying mindful and conscious, and focus on communication from your higher-self.

Call to Action and Your Commitment

Conscious communication is a critical step on the path of healing the planet, where individuals or groups can calmly settle their differences with words instead of violence, peace instead of war. This is what I believe is at stake.

For my part, I've committed to embracing the conscious mindset and it's already had a significant impact in my personal and professional life.

I practice with my husband, family, co-workers, and friends. As a result, I have some amazing, fulfilling relationships. When I encounter a conflict with someone, I do my best to remain conscious and use the tools to calmly create understanding between us. Each time I slip back into old patterns, I catch myself and return to being a *conscious communicator.*

I invite you to join me in this commitment to be a conscious communicator in each moment. We can use conscious communications to demonstrate a better way of communicating, bringing some clarity and sanity to the world. Together, we can move towards the tipping point of transforming communications on the planet. I believe we can be the generation that ushers in a wave of conscious communication for the next millennium and beyond.

I acknowledge you for reading this chapter and for the work you've already done in contribution to conscious communications.

The next time you have a conversation with someone who matters to you, remember to ask yourself, "Am I being a conscious communicator right now?"

To Contact Mary:

Email: mary@magneticpodium.com

Telephone: (617) 858-1466

Website: www.MagneticPodium.com

LinkedIn: www.linkedin.com/in/marycheyne

Twitter: twitter.com/Mary_Cheyne

Facebook: www.facebook.com/mary.cheyne

YouTube: www.youtube.com/user/MagneticPodium

Stephen Simpson, MD

Dr. Stephen Simpson is a Fellow of the Royal Society of Medicine, and Elite Performance Director. He regularly appears on TV and radio, and his clients include leading names from the diverse worlds of sport, business, the entertainment industries, and professional poker.

Dr. Simpson is also a best-selling author, actor, and presenter. As a feature writer for *The Best You* magazine, his articles appear regularly in leading newspapers and magazines.

Dr. Simpson has lived in war-torn Angola, the swamps of Nigeria, the steppes of Kazakhstan, and the deserts of Oman. As an international Medical and HR Director, he was privileged to work with many world leaders, including Bill Clinton, and was a task force member of the World Economic Forum, and Global Business Coalition.

During these exciting times, Dr. Simpson initiated medical programs in remote areas that continue to deliver high quality medical care to disadvantaged groups. These outreach programs received widespread international recognition and won prestigious awards. They are still used as case studies of best practice. The HIV programs alone have been instrumental in saving thousands of lives every year.

Full details of his articles, audiobooks, books, podcasts, and videos can be found on his website.

Get Lucky Now!

The Seven Secrets for Abundant Health, Wealth, and Happiness

By Stephen Simpson, MD

I am Stephen Simpson, a medical doctor, and Fellow of the Royal Society of Medicine. I have worked exclusively as an elite performance director for the last seven years. I present workshops all over the world and so can now predict the topics that resonate most deeply with delegates. These topics are usually related to the timeless trilogy of health, wealth, and happiness. I ask a series of questions from the stage to extract more detail. Then I add a magic word to the conversation. I ask quietly, 'Would you like to have more LUCK in your life?'

The atmosphere in the room becomes electrifying, as the delegates lean forward in their seats. This magic word that ignited the audience is 'luck'. Everybody wants to get lucky.

Is that possible? After you have read this book, you will decide.

I appear regularly on TV and radio, and my clients include leading names from the diverse worlds of sport, business, the entertainment industries, and professional poker.

I am also a best-selling author and presenter. As well as being a feature writer for *The Best You* magazine, my articles are published in leading newspapers and magazines.

I am not sharing this glitzy introduction with you to massage my ego, but for a far more important reason. Let me ask you a question.

Would you hire a financial advisor who clearly has difficulty meeting his or her mortgage payments?

Would you consult with a life coach who clearly has serious unresolved issues in their personal life?

Would you be prepared to make significant life changes for your abundant health, wealth, and happiness based on recommendations from a person who has not made their own abundant health, wealth, and happiness?

You would not, so now you will understand why I shared just a few details of my life with you. Even thinking about luck appears to ignite primeval emotions, or even obsessions. These are probably rooted deep in our reptilian brain. Yes, we all want more health, wealth, and happiness, but our overarching wish is fundamental. It is to be lucky.

Many of my clients have been hugely lucky, and I am going to share some of their lucky secrets so that you can get lucky too. One of them was so lucky that he won over a million dollars shortly after we worked together.

1. Goals

The first secret of success is to accurately identify your goals. The challenge is that most people do not really know what they want from life. They know what they think they want, but that is often not quite the same.

Mark Twain clearly observed a similar lack of clarity amongst his circle of acquaintances.

The Change[8]

'I can teach anybody how to get what they want out of life. The problem is that I can't find anybody who can tell me what they want.'

It is very easy to think of an impressive goal, but is it the correct one? Is it something you want to achieve, or something that parents, teachers, or friends have recommended?

When people follow their passion, they are rarely disappointed. These are the lucky people. How do you spend your money at present, after all the bills have been paid?

How do you spend your discretionary time? What activity makes time fly, fills you with deep contentment either during or afterwards, and, in a humble and grounded way, you know that you are rather good at?

So once you have decided on your real goal, the more different ways you can remind yourself of your goal each day, the more successful you are likely to be. There are many ways to do this. Examples include writing the goal on stickers and fixing them to the bathroom mirror, the refrigerator, using the goal as a screensaver on your computer, mobile phone, and alarm clock.

These actions direct your unconscious mind, and help to build a self-fulfilling prophecy. Also keep in mind that writing is the doing part of thinking, and is also a powerful connection to your unconscious mind.

Good intentioned thoughts often remain as good intentioned thoughts.

Spoken thoughts sometimes get done.

Written thoughts often lead to unimagined success.

When you share them with another person, the sky is the limit.

'A goal properly set is halfway reached.' - Abraham Lincoln

2. Confidence

This second secret is confidence and is extremely important in determining whether you will lead a lucky life. Fortunately, there are many ways to increase your confidence and self-esteem. The truth is that what goes on in your head will sooner or later come out in your life. Henry Ford expressed this succinctly, 'Whether you think you can or think you can't - you are right.'

One of the things that goes on in your head is a voice. It may be your own voice, or it may belong to somebody else. Often it is the voice of authority from the past, perhaps a teacher, or a parent.

This voice is your internal dialogue. Your mind is usually full with a constant chatter giving a running commentary of your life. Very often it slips out of the mouth, usually followed by an embarrassed pause. 'I was just talking to myself,' you mutter.

Adopt this mantra right now. Say it out aloud.

'From this moment forward, I will only say good things about myself.'

Follow this mantra for a week and you will start noticing how your mood and your luck have improved. Follow this mantra for a month and your friends and family will start asking what has changed in your life.

If you are concerned that you might lose out on learning from your mistakes or become arrogant, you can add the following words if you so wish.

'Fear not. I can trust family, friends, and the rest of the world to point out my mistakes. I do not need to give them any help.'

The Change[8]

This is another exercise that is well worth adopting. It is about remembering the good times. As with most things in life, it will require some preparation and effort on your part. However when compared to the size of the glittering prize out there it will be one of the best investments you have ever made.

A powerful starting point is to make this commitment. Write it down, and then you are much more likely to keep to it. Say it out aloud too, with conviction.

'From this moment forward, I will remember every good thing that happens to me.'

Unfortunately, most people have a brilliant memory for remembering all the things that went wrong, but struggle to think of the many good things that have gone right in their lives.

So when something goes well for you, wallow in the pleasure for a second or two longer than you ordinarily would, before allowing the memory to slip into your unconscious mind. If you can do this several times a day for a month, there will be a subtle change in your brain chemistry and outlook on life. You will notice the difference. Those closest to you will notice it more.

You can enhance this effect by subtly giving your brain another push in the right direction. When you have one of these pleasurable experiences, make sure that the memory is easy to retrieve by associating it with a physical anchor.

Some people touch their thumb and forefinger together to reinforce a happy memory. Others touch their ear or brush their trousers. Spend some time choosing yours. It should be discreet, but most importantly it should feel right with you.

Adopt this practice for a month, and the chances are that you will continue in the future. These anchors will soon become a seamless and automatic part of your life.

3. Make Magic Movies

A common characteristic of successful and lucky people is that they have a very clear picture in their head of what it is they wish to achieve. These are called visualizations.

Albert Einstein had magical visualizations too. He explained that most of his creative thoughts were in pictures, and that he rarely thought in words at all. This is proof that a picture, or visualization, is worth more than a thousand words.

You can create pictures in your mind too. It is even more powerful when you make your own movies in your head to reconstruct the success that you desire.

Great movie directors know the importance of creating vivid imagery using all our senses. These are our only information inputs from our environment. We have five senses; what we see, hear, feel, taste, and smell. Now it is time for you to direct your own movie. Make sure it is packed with detail relating to your five senses.

So let the cameras roll. Lie back, close your eyes, and imagine some success you have achieved in the future, perhaps a few months away. Then reflect on all the things that went right over the preceding months to position you for your success. You recognize that your processes were sound, and that your journey was a series of small steps, and not all of them were in the correct direction, or so it seemed at the time.

Your thoughts are interrupted as a journalist from the local paper approaches and asks you for the secret of the amazing improvement in your life. Could you pass on some tips that would interest and help her readers?

Pause for thought for a few seconds. Then share with her some of the most illuminating insights and suggestions that you found the most useful.

What you have done is change your perspective. You have permitted your brain to create a vivid movie of a positive outcome even though it is in the future. Furthermore, you have also changed your perspective by being the observer, and watching yourself behave with unconscious excellence in this movie.

4. Mindfulness

Our brains are very like computers. We can only handle so much information at any one time. When our brains are overloaded, they slow down, or even freeze, just like the dreaded PC 'blue screen of death.'

Computers work fastest when only one program is running. Our brains too work best when only a few programs are open.

So what does this have to do with getting lucky? A great deal. Spotting opportunities is a state of mind, and therefore dependent on how many things you are thinking about at any one time.

This is important because scientists have established that our brains can only handle seven packets of information at any one time. Once this limit is exceeded, the pure information becomes corrupted. So we miss opportunities, and we make bad decisions.

This is why we are most happy when we are totally absorbed in just one task. Time flies, the ego is for once subservient, and we become almost totally unaware of our environment.

However, the challenge is that we have never been so surrounded by so much up-to-the-second information. This information bombards us from TV, radio, newspapers, social media, breaking news, text messages, telephones, diary reminders, and emails. So if you want to find the optimum state of mind to get lucky, how can you limit the information you allow in?

Just switch these distractions off, at least while you are doing something else. There is nothing more certain to break a flowing presentation, the creation of a beautiful work of art, or the straight flight of an arrow than a single thought. Quite simply, multitasking does not work.

'It is only when we silent the blaring sounds of our daily existence that we can finally hear the whispers of truth that life reveals to us, as it stands knocking on the doorsteps of our hearts.' K.T. Jong

5. The Three H's

The three H's of Hypnosis, Heartmath, and Havening are the most powerful weapons in my armory. Used together, they have helped to produce some incredible results in my clients. One of the most notable examples is a professional poker player who won over $1 million shortly after our sessions together. Another golf client scored three holes-in-one in just six months. The odds against this happening are astronomical.

All three of these techniques have their supporters and sceptics. The science to support each of them is incomplete, and sometimes controversial. All I know is that I practice these techniques daily, and they work well for me and my clients too. Here is a little more information about these techniques.

We are surrounded by examples of hypnosis. Everybody can be a hypnotist. One of the best examples is the natural way that mothers soothe their troubled child. Many advertisements that we see on TV are also hypnotic, whether their creators know this or not.

Havening is a newer technique which at its simplest level is described as a psycho sensory technique. Again, a transfer of energy occurs in some subtle way. Possibly its origins also go much further back in time. This technique is particularly effective for treating post-traumatic stress disorder, and works in the deep reptilian part of the brain known as the amygdala.

Again, mothers are often perfect examples to observe when they unconsciously use the havening touch with their children. They did not need to read a book to learn this technique or take a course. It is a natural reflex to comfort another person.

Heartmath is also a relatively new technique, and is a form of meditation. The benefits of regular meditation are well established in science. They include reducing anxiety, high blood pressure, and even cancer.

Heartmath is being used increasingly in professional sports and in schools to enhance performance and create the ideal mental state. The heart contains large amounts of nerves. It was thought that these nerves responded to stimulation from the brain. Now it is known that the reverse is often true. The impulses from the heart control the brain. This might explain why people use the expression. 'I knew in my head that this was the right decision, but in my heart I knew it was wrong.'

It is possible that all three different techniques are closely related. During our evolution, the larynx and its related structures that enabled us to speak were one of our final developments. Clearly people were able to communicate with each other long before speech evolved. They did so by using a variety of sounds, postures, and different forms of touch. Just as animals have always done, which might explain why they have less communication problems than we do.

6. The Luck Magnet

Everybody wants more luck in their life. Is this possible?

The truth is that it is possible and there are some very logical reasons to explain why this is so. There are also some extremely illogical reasons, and these are more difficult to explain.

I spoke to many people about luck whilst researching my latest book, *Get Lucky Now!* An expression that I heard many times was 'the harder I work the luckier I get'.

This is true, because everything in life has to be worked at. Very few people achieve great success without a great deal of effort. However there are many people who spend their whole lives working very hard and have very little luck and success to show for it. Compared to some people who work a lot less and yet have a lot more luck.

Researchers have identified a consistent pattern amongst people who lead a lucky life. They are often extrovert and attract many friends. They have large social networks and so are often the first person to hear of new opportunities.

They also have a relaxed attitude to life and so are more likely to see all of the options available to them. An anxious person has their focus on internal rather than external issues, and so they never recognize these opportunities.

However, even lucky people face adversity at some point in their life and their attitude to it is very different from the unlucky population. They are convinced that however bad things look, all will work out for the best. They will be stronger for it. They do not blame themselves or others for their misfortune and move on to the future far more rapidly than other people.

Whereas unlucky people give up in the face of adversity. Sometimes when they are a lot closer to their goal than they realize.

7. Magic

These are just a few of the magical origins of luck. One definition of magic is the power of apparently influencing events by using mysterious or supernatural forces.

Carl Jung viewed luck as synchronicity. He described luck as a meaningful coincidence. So he believed that luck is not random. This is very different to the *Webster* definition of luck, which is a purposeless unpredictable and uncontrollable that shapes events favorably or unfavorably for an individual, group, or cause.

Jung was so fascinated by synchronicity that he wrote a paper about it, and even held long conversations with Einstein.

Another fascinating aspect of luck is its connection to intuition. There is much that we can do to improve our intuition. All of the secrets of success that I have described develop intuition skills.

Often people talk about having gut feelings and lucky people tend to follow them. Most people's conscious mind is so busy that there is no way for the unconscious mind to speak and to be heard. So I spend a lot of time with my clients teaching them meditation skills and using techniques such as hypnosis, havening and heartmath, as mentioned in the previous section.

It is beyond the scope of this chapter to discuss the magic associated with quantum, string, and relativity theory, but one day some person will unify these conflicting theories.

Let us hope that it will be a magically lucky day for us all.

To Contact Stephen:

Website: www.drstephensimpson.com

Email: doc@drstephensimpson.com

Amazon Author Page:

www.amazon.co.uk/Dr-Stephen-Simpson/e/B004S71PJG/ref=ntt_dp_epwbk_0

YouTube Channel:
www.youtube.com/channel/UCI3XSk8PDtvdxNd5P7k5IUg

Nancy Proffitt

Nancy Proffitt, President of Proffitt Management Solutions, is a certified business coach committed to enhancing the leadership competencies of individuals and corporate leaders. We help businesses develop plans and identify processes which increase efficiency while developing the people skills to be successful.

Our approach will strengthen management skills, build collaboration, improve communication, and increase productivity throughout the organization.

Our clients are able to prepare effectively for the future, improve employee performance, and provide the best customer service to maintain measureable profitable results.

Nancy Proffitt is a national business coach, author, and keynote speaker. Her 20 years in senior management with FedEx Corporation, BME, MBA in Finance and Operations, and certification in Business Coaching are just a few of her many qualifications that set her apart and earned her recognition as a "TOP 100 Leader in Fortune Global100 Business".

- Executive Board for Leadership Palm Beach County
- Board of Directors for Girls Scouts SE Florida
- Business Person of the Year – Boca Raton Chamber of Commerce
- National Speaker Association
- National Association of Women MBA's

The Change[8]

- Lifetime member of Girl Scouts of America
- Cambridge Who's Who of Executives
- WBENC Certified Woman Owned Business

Managing Change by Changing Minds

By Nancy Proffitt

Change is inevitable, not only in organizations but everywhere. Without change we stagnate and become irrelevant as a business, a team, or a person. The result of not changing is that our competition and our customers leave us behind. So why is changing people's behaviors one of the most important challenges for business leaders competing in unpredictable environments? There are a huge number of books available about change management – all with competing theories, ideas, and suggestions about how to do it, get our people on board, and make the change sustainable. Given all this information, why is it that so many of our organizational change initiatives fail?

The dirty little secret is we *can't* change others; we can only change *our* approach to create the change we want to see – the change must happen within ourselves first. To initiate behavioral changes in others, they must see a clear and compelling reason to change—in other words, we must change their minds. How do we do that? By understanding what change management means, defining the three common change reactions, and developing a roadmap for change.

Let's first understand what managing change really means. We are changing people's minds about the way things are done—not trying to change the person.

The Change[8]

The formal definition of change management is "coordinating a number of activities and inter-relationships so that the organization can survive and benefit from the process of change." A more common explanation for managing change is simply the process of planning and implementing change in organizations in such a way as to minimize employee resistance and cost to the organization while simultaneously maximizing the effectiveness of the change effort. Change is supposed to produce improvement—plain and simple. Change should never happen for the sake of change. Instead, we start with a clear outcome, and then develop a well-thought-out plan with measurements to determine progress toward the desired outcome.

Effectively managing change is less about the actual event itself and more about understanding the emotional component human beings experience when going through any change process. Effective leaders focus on the *why* and clearly and consistently articulate this key element when managing change. They do it in a way so people want to become a part of making the change happen – they motivate people to do what is needed instead of just going through the motions.

Once people understand the *why,* then leaders can foster the move towards a successful outcome by developing a clear roadmap for implementation. The plan should outline what is actually changing (and what isn't), who will be affected, and how will the process work. Communication is especially critical throughout the roll-out of the plan so everyone clearly understands his or her role in the process, the expectations the manager has about the functions of those roles, and the benefits to be realized from the change itself.

But effective managers also need to be aware of people's perceptions of change initiatives.

When thinking about change in general, consider the range of emotions people can have when faced with having to make changes. Consider the changes you have experienced at work from processes, to assignments, to personnel changes. How did you feel? Also keep in mind that some changes are clearly positive, like getting a promotion and some are clearly negative, like a demotion or downsizing. There are also changes that we may perceive as "neutral," but others see as threatening. A new IT process, for example, can cause stakeholders to be concerned about their new role, how they will interact with others, and their status in the organization.

Words or phrases that people use reflect their feelings toward change. Be aware that the following words reflect positive feelings: improvement, opportunity, upgrades, progress, or expansion. Some terms that come to mind that show a negative perspective might be: uncomfortable, stress, unknown, fear, difficult, or never works.

So, why do we need to identify the range of emotions and how does this help us? First, it will help us identify where on the continuum of reactions our employees are. Second, consider that many of the negative reactions to change are really rooted in fear of the unknown.

Let's use a simple example: Wherever you are right now, try this short, easy experiment: I want you to cross your arms. My operational definition of "crossed" is folding your arms together, as if you were bored or waiting for something. How does that feel? Now fold your arms the other way, reversed of what you just performed. I guarantee that 90 percent of us will struggle with it. When people initially cross their arms, they do so naturally, without even thinking about it. When they are asked to fold them the other way they, for the most part, have to stop, refold their arms again and then try to figure out which arm was on top, which arm moves first, and so on.

How did it feel when you crossed your arms the other way? Did it come naturally or did you have to stop and think about it? Were you comfortable with doing this differently from your normal process? Of course not! It took time to think it through and then within even seconds, you wanted to put your arms down and refold them the "old" way which was more comfortable. This reaction to simply folding your arms differently is exactly what people experience when asked to make a change at work.

How many people love to change—in fact, the more change the better? Not the majority! A good change manager knows you don't have to love change to lead it effectively. In general, why do you think people are resistant to change? Maybe it's about uncharted terrain, it's stressful, or it may require them to work more. If the change process isn't handled effectively, the situation may become worse than before. Many people subscribe to the "if it ain't broken, then don't fix it" philosophy and their past experiences have shown there are no guarantees that things will improve.

Rick Maurer, a change agent and author of *Beyond the Wall of Resistance*, states when changes fail, people often grow cynical. We may hear things such as "Here we go again…" or "Here comes another flavor of the month" or "We're lying low until this fad blows over."

Research from the *Prosci 2012 Best Practices in Change Management Benchmarking Report* has shown with effective change management, 95% of employee's reported achieving the objectives of change and 71% also reported the change stayed on schedule – remember the plan? On the other hand, when change was not managed effectively, only 16% of the people thought the objectives had been met or the change plan or the change stayed on schedule.

Effective leaders help others to understand the necessity of change, help them see a vision of improvement because of the change, and help them stay on track throughout the process.

One key task of managing change initiatives is overcoming people's resistance to change. Managing change is also managing people's fears and attitude. Change is natural and good, but people's reaction to change is sometimes unpredictable and can even be irrational. People's reactions can be managed if it's done the right way. Good managers are continually learning new ways to manage the varied reactions employees may have. Professor Howard Gardner, expert mind researcher, has determined mind changing is sometimes more likely to occur when resources and rewards (positive reinforcement) are made available.

Since managing reactions and resistance are keys to successful outcomes, let's take a look at three common types of reaction: Supportive, Neutral, and Resistant. But let's be clear - responses to organizational change vary widely among people. Some support the change and get on board fairly quickly, others remain neutral, and some come in and go out kicking with resistance in an almost knee-jerk manner.

We'll first talk about those who are supportive of the change—they have an attitude of "what's the worst that can happen?" It does not take a lot for them to change their mindset and see the benefits and they are often the ones who help change happen. Supportive people take personal responsibility for initiating improvements. They're usually comfortable straying from the status quo and often anticipate the need for change. These folks keep the future in mind and know that change is necessary to maintain a competitive edge and offer the most innovation for customers. Having those people on the team is critical to motivating others and they become problem solvers to make change work. An additional characteristic of people who are more supportive of change is that they are comfortable with

The Change[8]

assessing their own feelings and reactions. They're quick to understand the "What is in it for me?" and the "How will it affect me and how can I make this a win?"

Even if a person is not happy about a change, those who are supportive about the change will look for ways to make it work. People who are supportive of change have found a personal connection to the change in their work lives. They can see the benefit of the change for themselves. Supportive people may not love change, but they will do what they need to in order to support it. For example, an employee may not be happy about their work station being moved to another location. But despite not being happy about it, they pack up their boxes and offer to help clean the new area before the final move into their new place.

Others will know that *you* are supportive of change if you are just that: supportive. You don't have to like the change, either, but you do have to be more than accepting – you need to support it wholeheartedly and show by your behavior that you believe in the benefits.

Next, let's look at the "Neutrals." These I call the "fence sitters." They don't say "yeah" or "nay" because they are waiting to see the consequences of the change. If the outcome is good, they'll be the first to say, "I knew it would work." Conversely, if the situation does not work well, they'll quickly pipe up, "I knew this wouldn't work!" or "I figured so, that's why I didn't support it."

Agreeing without commitment is a telltale sign of the neutral. Some folks go with the flow. They have the attitude of "it is what it is." These people don't endorse or disagree with the change. Their attitude is simply that there is nothing they can do to change what is happening, so they will just go with it for now. This is the "whatever" group. If they disagree, they don't overreact and often don't even share their thoughts with others. They often agree with the supporter if no one is around or agree with the resister when no one is listening. Again, this fence-sitting posture only slows the process for implementing the necessary change.

Finally, we have those who actively or passively resist change. They are often fearful of change and resist because of past experiences where change created more work or an uncomfortable situation. Their resistance may also stem from their fear of failure. They're not certain they can perform up to standards in a new situation. After all, it's better to know the devil they have than the devil they don't know. Instead of taking responsibility for their own reactions, resisters often find ways to find fault and stand in the way of the supporters or fence sitters. By passively resisting change, people's behavior may manifest itself by denying they are opposed and unsupportive, yet they are not on board and are quietly subversive in their resistance. The resister may instead decide to be overt in their actions by protesting publically. It may look like defiance. Sabotaging the efforts of those wishing to effect constructive change is destructive and this person who disagrees with change will work to make the initiative fail so they can be right.

What can we do to get others to change their minds and understand that not all change is bad? The most important aspect for a leader to consider is that they have to become the change agent. A change agent has a positive attitude about the changes needed and knows that each person within the organization may have a different response because each person is a product of their own life experiences. It is important when asking others to do something differently that we address it through *their* filter, not ours. What's comfortable to us may not be so with others.

So how then do we become the change agents who can implement transformation effectively? A good change agent understands there are three key drivers to affecting positive change: empathy, communication, and contribution.

EMPATHY - Empathy is the ability to understand and share the feelings of another. People's reactions to change are not always logical. An individual's needs at the time take precedence over everything else in their decision to adapt to change. Resist the reaction to downplay someone's response as silly or nonsense. A good manager realizes where people are coming from and they make a concerted effort to understand others' reactions. It doesn't mean they agree—they simply accept the reaction. Effective change management requires empathetic insight into others' behavioral styles, needs, and feelings. Resist the temptation to judge others based on their reactions to the news of change because chances are we don't know what may be driving that behavior. Again, unsatisfactory prior experiences and harsh judgment may be the very reason people react the way they do to change. When we listen for *intent* and not *content*, we have a better chance to "hear" the real reasons for their reactions to change. This is the time to ask more probing questions, which can lead to a more trusting relationship. During periods of change people want to know they are still valued. By exhibiting genuine empathy, a manager can build and solidify relationships to effect a more positive outcome.

COMMUNICATION - Another element of change management often overlooked is the importance of good communication. In times of change and uncertainty, the need for constant and consistent communication is paramount. Keeping communication lines open for questions, discussion, and disagreement is critical to gaining buy-in. People want to know who'll be directing the change and who'll be affected – and how. They want to know what information is available—so tell them what you know and be sure it's factual. Avoid the "rumor highway" by communicating regularly throughout the process and squashing rumors as they start. This can be difficult, but know that finding the right time and right place to disseminate information is as important as the information itself.

This brings us to the most critical piece of communication—the **WHY**. If people know the real reason why a change is necessary, they are often much more willing to accept the alteration to the norm. Most people will be more likely to respond positively to change if they believe the reasons are valid and truthful. Employees are adults—they can handle the truth if it is delivered with empathy and done so effectively. Introduce new ideas into the mainstream without excessive use of authority. Some managers are just "tellers"—that is not communication. Good leaders deliver honest reasonable communication often—and listen often!

CONTRIBUTION- The third component of effective change management is contribution. Change feels more natural when you have engagement at all levels. People accept change when they can be a part of the change. People want to participate in the process so they don't become a victim of the process. A participatory setting is exactly the type of work environment a good change agent creates. People have a chance to give opinions, formulate plans, and control the process when given the opportunity to participate. After all, who does the change affect the most? This is an opportunity to find out from employees what might work or not, or a better way for the process to be implemented.

Do not demand people participate when asking for input and involvement. Not everyone is comfortable giving opinions until they know they'll be accepted or that constructive feedback is done so in a professional manner. All ideas will not be good ideas. Let them know up front why an idea may not work. Create an environment in which the idea, not the person delivering the idea, may be the concern. A different way to negate an idea is to ask the person to describe how his or her idea would fit in the process and if it isn't a good way to go, they will often make that discovery on their own once they talk through the process. Creating a safe environment for ideas and input to be shared freely is fundamental to structuring a good participation model.

When more people contribute to finding solutions, communicating well, and helping each other, there is a better chance of achieving real behavioral change. To ensure everyone can see progress, management must provide positive reinforcement to keep people motivated and engaged, to encourage people to remain supportive of the change, and to make sure they're onboard with the desired outcomes.

Good change agents remain cognizant of people's emotional reaction to changes and understand their need to be involved in the change process. Delivering the same content in multiple ways is a powerful way to change people's minds. There is no one way to communicate—written or spoken—a good manager creates an image of what the end result will be so people will be more likely to accept that change is inevitable.

In summary, changing minds is not always easy, but there are clear methods for increasing the probability of effecting real change if we develop an appropriate change initiative roadmap, acknowledge different reactions to change initiatives, and implement the process using the tools of empathy, communication, and contribution. Remember: we are not changing people—we are changing people's minds to produce a better result.

To Contact Nancy:

www.proffittmanagement.com

www.linkedin.com/in/nancyproffitt

www.facebook.com/ProffittManagementSolutions

twitter.com/nancyproffitt

561-582-6060

Marcus Cox

Marcus was a "pretty normal guy" until he was in a horrendous car accident that left him in a coma and he "crossed over to the other side." The journey through a long recovery and deep depression turned out to be one of his greatest blessings as it led him on a journey to understand what life is really about, how to connect with his higher self, and help others do the same.

Studying under Yoga Masters and Gurus in India and Sri Lanka, Marcus discovered some ancient consciousness expanding methods, including deep meditation, energy transmutation, Lucid Dreaming, and tapping into the Superconscious self that transforms the core of our lives.

During this time, Marcus witnessed a Tsunami of "coincidences" where everything falls in line, or what many people would call miracles. He observed a principle was at work that was beyond normal reasoning and included a feeling of continual inspiration accompanied by an endless chain of "Aha moments." He also marveled at how living in this inspired state obliterated obstacles and barriers to living a limitless life.

Marcus is now helping others reset their lives and live the abundant life that is everyone's birthright.

Going Beyond the Box

By Marcus Cox

"You must be the change you want to see in the world" – Mahatma Gandhi

True change is a gift that can open up a life of Limitless possibilities, but we must first go beyond the box of limitations that hold us back. Embracing true change can be challenging and there are "many paths up the mountain." This story is about my path and my wish is that it inspires you to embrace your truth and go beyond the box!

Have you ever had an "Aha!" moment? What did you observe before that wonderful moment arrived? Was it the result of laborious thinking where you had been "trying to figure something out" or did the understanding just "pop into your head" and make perfect sense? It popped, didn't it! It felt like magic and you "just knew it was right."

How about that sort of childlike joy and inquisitive posture that comes with that Aha Moment – it feels good, does it not?

Have you ever fallen in love? Do you remember the magic and incredible feelings you shared? There is nothing quite like that feeling and it transcends logic; it can be crazy good with no thinking required.

Have you traveled to foreign lands and met people that feel like long lost family members, but you technically do not know them or speak their language? Do you remember the shared comradery that transcended logic and left you with magic memories?

If you have had any of these experiences, then you know how it feels to go beyond the box!

The Box That Limits Our Lives

So what is this "box" or barrier that prevents us from being inspired or in-spirit?

It is our Ego and *Webster's Dictionary* describes the "ego" as "the opinion you have of yourself," but it is a lot deeper than that! The opinion you have is also an accumulation of opinions formed by "other people" who think you should act, look, and be a certain way. These opinions have been accumulating since you learned your name and started thinking about who and what you are, not to mention that nagging question "why"!

This box of opinioned knowledge keeps you from feeling connected with the Divine and living the Limitless life you deserve – one of no doubt or fear. Are you ready to Go Beyond the Box once and for all?

"Opinionated knowledge is only barrier to the Superconscious." – Swami Subramuniya

My personal journey of going beyond this box is pretty out there and is a story I have been afraid to tell because I was worried "what people would think"! Well, it is my time to speak my truth and not care what "they think" – here goes!

"The truth shall set you free." — John 8:38

When I grew up, I didn't have a 50-hour playlist of Tony Robbins webinars on YouTube to overcome my hang-ups and crippling self-doubts, or was able to watch Dr. Wayne Dyer on *Oprah* as they expound breathtaking truths from the *Tao Te Ching*, or order books like Jim Britt's *Rings of Truth* from Amazon.com and have it delivered to my door. Back then, we didn't have global broadcasts in multiple languages talking about "The New Earth, Awakening to your life's purpose" on EckhartTolle.TV, or movies like *What the Bleep Do We Know* showing how quantum physics proves that light, or pure energy, is all there is.

My path was different…

I might have been "normal" (or so it would seem) and had a "normal life," but in 1968, I basically died and crossed over to the other side! Like most kids, I had totally bought into the Matrix and was lusting toward being popular, having great adventures, making a lot of money, and living life in style. Like most of us, I had been brainwashed to believe making a lot of money and having a lot of stuff was the key to happiness, and you had to get a good education and work hard so you could have more stuff.

Fortunately (life's lessons never seem fortunate at the time), on the last day of summer vacation, I was with some friends going 90 mph on a gravel road (you ever have someone show off while you are a helpless passenger?). When we careened into the ditch, hit a boulder, and rolled several times, they said I must have gone 100 feet in the air after I took the windshield out with my head!

Crossing over to the Other Side

What I remember next was the classic "crossing over" story where I was in a tunnel of light, saw "light beings" or Celestials at the other end, and they were beckoning me to join them. My coma lasted 10 days and I alternated between floating on the ceiling of my hospital room, looking down at my wrecked body with all these tubes connected, and being in the tunnel of light. Trust me, the light was MUCH more attractive than that poor guy in the hospital room.

However, on the 10th day, I opened my eyes to see a nurse standing over me and heard machines pumping to keep me alive – I was back!

This crossing over stuff may sound weird to you, but if you do some research, it is not so weird anymore! Try the following "out of the box" exercise and see for yourself.

Goggle search on the following people's names, in quotes, and "Near Death" in quotes:

1. "Anita Moorjani" + "Near Death" – you will love Anita's story. After battling cancer and withering to 85 pounds, Anita went into a coma, crossed over to the other side, and then came back like I did. She not only came back from the other side, but her cancerous tumors went away! Anita is now helping a lot of people "go beyond the box" and has been interviewed by famous talk show hosts like Maria Shriver and was also interviewed on the *Today* show (she also wrote a book titled *Dying to Be Me* with a foreword by Dr. Wayne Dyer, one of my favorite authors).

2. "Dr. Steven Greer" + "Near Death" and watch his YouTube video on how he died and came back when he was 17 years old (he also explains it in his book *Hidden Truth Forbidden Knowledge* starting on page 20). If you REALLY want to test your ability to go beyond your box or belief structure, Google search "Congress UFO Secret Meeting" on YouTube and watch Dr. Greer, several senators, astronauts, scientists, and others testify about the UFO presence on Earth.

These are just two stories, but they are my favorites and they may help you discover this process of observing your reaction, opening your mind, and going beyond your "box of preconceived ideas" — aka opinionated knowledge. The next couple of stories are samples of tapping into the superconscious or Limitless self and the new energies that you can have access to.

3. "Joseph Pierce Farrell" is known for healing by intention, using his mind to manifest changes in bone structure (watch the videos on his work), remove inoperable cancer tumors, heal broken bones, and even do facial remolding where multiple surgeries had failed (check out the video by Sammy, one of his patients who plastic surgeons had given up on).

NOTE: Joseph said he wasted many years in a prestigious job on Wall Street after his high school guidance counselor had told him he was too stupid to be a doctor. Doing what "they thought" he should be doing, he pursued a career on Wall Street and did very well – at least financially that is. However, he wanted to be a healer and became very miserable. In his book *Manifesting Michelangelo*, he likened his Wall Street job to selling his soul to the devil!

After quitting his lucrative job and ignoring what "they thought he should be doing," he has been one of the leading doctors in alternative health care, and is helping others tap into their Divinity.

Dr. Richard Bartlett (my wife and I have been to his seminars – TOTALLY out of the box) described how this Superconscious energy healing works in his book *The Physics of Miracles*:

"These spiritual and energetic technologies have been around for maybe two thousand years, and they possess a really big morphic field that almost no one is tapping into."

As you can see, tapping into other realities and embracing life transforming change could possibly make YOU one of the great contributors in our time too. We all have this potential inside of us, but to tap into it we must go beyond the ego jail and box of opinions – can you do (be) this?

Forget what "they say" and act consciously with courage! It is time to listen to your heart!

Observe your thoughts instead of identifying with them.

Observe your thoughts now – did you feel uncomfortable having your "belief structure" challenged? Did you react or get emotional about going beyond the box of "normal" or what you think is normal? Is it what you truly believe is normal or are you trying to fit in with what "they think" is normal and not look weird?

Were you able to observe your reactions or did you buy into it and get emotional with a tightening at the navel? If you "witnessed" your thoughts and reactions and noted rather than reacted to them, then congratulations – you just witnessed how to Go Beyond the Box!

Having an open mind is the first phase of this wondrous process…

"To Hold the hand must first be Open." – Lao Tzu

Melting the Box

When I came out of that 10-day coma, I was one of the most confused people on the planet (concussions can do that!). Within a week of being released, I continued my pain med addiction and graduated to injecting heavier drugs like crystal meth and heroin. The ensuing depression and "woe is me" or victim consciousness totally consumed me and I felt a separateness and loneliness as never before. I even tried committing suicide (what a waste of precious life that would have been)!

Going further into darkness, I quit school (grade 10) and ran away from home (high on heroin) to Vancouver, B.C. - a 1,000 miles through snow and ice to arrive at my new home—Vancouver's tenderloin district (rough area!). Besides being robbed at gunpoint and other scary stuff totally outside my comfort zone, I learned how to be resourceful, keep from freezing to death, not starve, and get a hands-on feel for what living on the street is like. Suffering is a powerful teacher and after 6 months of it, I surrendered my

The Change[8]

independence and pride and returned home to my parents to try and work things out.

What happened next was magic!

"That which is Called the Tao Is Not the Tao." – Lao Tzu

Have you ever read the *Tao Te Ching*? My brother had just come home from a trip to California and had a translation of the *Tao Te Ching* with him. He also had a bag of super potent LSD called Strawberry Ripple and told me he had seen the white light! I discovered the author, Dr. Timothy Leary, had led a group of consciousness researchers (Baba Ram Dass or Dr. Richard Alpert was one of them) at Harvard University and published this and other books on how LSD (nicknamed "acid") altered states of awareness. Of course, coming back from the other side made me the perfect candidate, so for the next 3 months I meditated on each "Psychedelic Prayer" while on LSD – daily!

I "Watched quietly while the 10,000 things came to life and returned to the source" (Tao), and "floated freely" without a body and traversed the Chakras as described in his book. A profound process awakened within me and what began as a lot of hallucinations and sensory explosion (Leary calls this a chaos of potentiality) turned to wonderment and profound cognitions as each prayer or verse of the *Tao Te Ching* revealed inner "light realms" or planes of consciousness.

After months of "consciousness expansion," I assumed what some yogis call "the witness position" and became an observer vs "the doer," or "detached awareness from that which it is aware of." Dropping acid is like mounting twin turbo chargers on your cognitive "Grok" engine and watching your thoughts melt in breathtaking sensible senselessness. In one of my favorite Prayers, it reads "See each part join the whole" and I experienced this in real time as my confusion of being a separate self merged with pure energy or Tao. As the forward in the book reads:

"The theory is simple: consciousness is energy received by structure."

All the "parts" or concepts of who or what I was were melted into "the light" or pure energy accompanied by heart melting compassion and love for all the crazy notions I had about who I thought I was. I had compassion for myself and everyone I'd known, and I understood why Jesus said "Forgive them for they know not what they do." From my Christian background, I saw this astonishing state of total connectivity as "Heaven on Earth" or "Thy kingdom come, thy will be done, on Earth as it is in Heaven." I could see how my ego-I had cut me off from the Divine and shut down the flow of harmony or love-bliss that is our true nature. When the thinking mind subsided and there was no interpretation or categorization of anything, there was only stillness, or Tao.

There were moments when I would lay down and dissolve into the stillness, all I could see was light, eyes opened or closed. Famous quotes drifted through my mind and had profound meaning:

"To Be or Not to Be – that is the question." - William Shakespeare

"Be Still and Know That I am God." – the Bible

"Just Be Here Now." – Baba Ram Dass

This falling into the light and merged state I became is called Samadhi in the Yoga traditions and it supposedly requires lifetimes of Sadhana or spiritual practice (when I was in India, my Guru would later tell me LSD was like being on an elevator and the door opens into the light realm temporarily and you feel like you have arrived - then the door closes, the elevator goes back down to good old ordinary you. He was right!).

The Change[8]

The Teacher Appears

After "blowing my mind" as we called it in the '60s and discovering how total surrender of the thought-based self leads to superconsciousness/love/light and a Tsunami of synchronistic "coincidences" (everything falls in place and miracles happen!) the next phase was to "Be Here Now" without LSD.

When my first teacher appeared, I was living with my brother in Vancouver and we were meditating and studying Eckankar, "The Ancient Science of Soul Travel." One Eckankar book, *The Tiger's Fang*, really had my attention. It was about the Guru's travels through the Inner planes (Astral, Causal, Supra Causal, Sach Kand) with his Guru, a story much like Yogananda tells in his book *Autobiography of a Yogi*, and I wanted to travel this path also. When the Guru came to Vancouver, we met in his hotel room, sat across from each other, and he instructed me what to do (or rather "be").

At the exact second I was out of my body in the corner of the room, he said sweetly "There you are." I immediately thought "How does he know I am out of my body" and I was immediately back in my body and sitting in the chair again – and I thought I was an advanced practitioner! Though I was saddened to be back in my body so fast, I was overwhelmed with joy and gratitude for sharing this moment with my teacher and knowing without a doubt I was not stark raving mad for believing in all this Guru stuff.

The room turned to light for what seemed hours as we meditated together.

At the end of our meeting, I asked him what my next step should be, and he said with a smile, "You should go back to school now." I wondered how he knew I was a dropout!

Taking his advice, I returned to high school and for the next seven years I witnessed a Tsunami of "coincidences" and auspicious events and pilgrimaged through 17 countries with my next teacher, Swami Subramuniya. I wound up renouncing my worldly possessions and joined his Monastic Order in Sri Lanka to live what I believed was the only thing in life that mattered – becoming one with God. As an adept at Ashtanga Yoga, I led groups of students on Yoga retreats in the jungles and deserts, but more importantly learned to go beyond myself or the Ego-I.

Monasteries are rarified environments and meditations are deep – it was a gift to serve!

It has been over 40 years since leaving the Monastery, but the Tsunami of "coincidences" and auspicious events have returned!

Having my chapter go into the 8th edition of *The Change* Series Books is interesting – the number 8 stands for Infinity and Infinity is truly beyond the box! It is also interesting my company logo is the number 8 on its side and that logo is on everything I sell. Another interesting thing is my company's motto is "To Unleash the Human Potential for Good" – and what do you think this book is about?

Coincidence? (LOL)

Our Invitation

My wife and I live on a mountainside and network with the world through webinars, Google Hangouts, podcasts, and videos, and are dedicated to helping our global family go beyond the box! Join us for some excellent "Reality Hacking" as we help you tap into your higher self and live a Superconscious life.

To Contact Marcus:

Our Blog on how to reboot your life: www.GoingBeyondTheBox.com

Our Networking Blog: www.MountainNetworker.com

Email: marcus@MountainNetworker.com

Phone: (707) 226-6313

Skype: marcus10086

Tom Erik Green

Tom Erik Green, is the founder and co-owner of PlusVendor AS. As a professional psychologist, he has lectured at international conferences on personality development, and has authored several scientific papers in international journals. Green started to develop the PlusCode concept in the early '90s from his psychotherapeutic practice and personal experience as a person who stutters. He struggled with stuttering from the age of seven. Tom was unable to speak fluently in the classroom as well as in ordinary social settings, and was drained of all self-confidence, not knowing how to become the person he longed to be—until he applied the methods outlined in this chapter.

ThePlusCode ®

Change and the Image You Hold In Your Mind

By Tom Erik Green

I'm honored that you are reading this chapter. Curiosity places us in situations that encourages change and the search for our best is deeply motivated by responsibility and respect. As a psychotherapist, it's clear that change is inevitable for clients when they are curious about what life requires of them in all sorts of situations—even those that are adverse. Adversity is life's way of helping you to seek the meaning of your existence.

> "Ultimately, man should not ask what the meaning of his life is, but rather must recognize that it is he who is asked." — Viktor E. Frankl, *Man's Search for Meaning*

Curiosity will drive you to search for answers, and the language you use will determine how you navigate in a responsible manner in regard to your best. The mission of this chapter is to propose a philosophy for successful navigation, and to provide you with a preliminary platform of concepts and terms to which you can return to gain strength—even in facing the toughest question that life asks us.

So, what seems to be needed is a philosophy of the mind, or a coding system, to organize our reactions to adverse situations, in light of our capacities and the intelligence of our life stream, which I refer to as your "Plus."

I compare the undertaking of finding the answers to life's questions and change to taking an exam in an unfamiliar subject. This analogy resonates with many of my clients who are looking for solutions to their problems. The adverse situations they find themselves in can often be described as a consequence of not being aware of their inherent potential. Therefore, they are unable to take advantage of their inner strength.

Another analogy that resonates has to do with personal growth, a subject we should be focused on throughout our lives instead of merely focusing on conquering our fears—which can illuminate our lack of ability rather than our failure to use these abilities.

To illustrate, imagine the blueprint of a beautiful tree, present in the kernel of a seed. Now imagine your own blueprint of everything you're capable of representing, which dwells within every single cell of your body. Your body is more capable than your conscious mind of representing your blueprint to the world. Your blueprint consists of all you are able to experience—love, respect, freedom, passion, enthusiasm, success, and all of our other personality traits.

Your limiting thoughts run the risk of hindering your potential. However, when you engage in a more positive dialogue with your "Plus," you can avoid many problems. This contact with your Plus enables you to discover the hidden resources and talents within, making it possible to charge yourself in every situation. You will now attract and manifest what you previously had only dreamt about.

So let's dive in together, highlight the "Plus" philosophy and some of its related terms and concepts, and build a preliminary system to help you uncover the opportunities you have to figure out your path to personal development and growth, and create the life you and your family deserve.

The Change[8]

What Is Your Potential?

In order to take advantage of your own potential for change, it is important to first be able to recognize it. Many people walk around filled with doubt about their own potential, skills, and abilities. How then are we supposed to believe we have a potential at all to build on and to create the life we want? Others do have a lot of evidence of their skills and abilities, but still feel like they do not have a direction in their life that reflects their true self. Let me illustrate with the story of Susan.

Susan was a thirty-five-year-old woman who had spent the last decade and a half pursuing several degrees at various universities. By the time we met, she had two Masters and a PhD, but no direction or passion in her life.

"I believed all this education would lead me to discover my path in life, but instead, with each degree, I only felt more disillusioned and lost. Now I'm not even sure what it is I want to contribute to the world or what it is I truly care about."

As she spoke, the light in her eyes was dim, and her voice was flat and muted. I had to lean forward to better get a sense of who Susan was, and utilize my intuition. I told her directly, "What you present to me is not the person I see."

She was quiet for a while as though she was not interested in my assessment, but after a second she continued talking. I gently interrupted her once more and said that she didn't seem interested in my assessment.

"I heard what you said, but I don't know how to respond."

I replied in an understanding way, "I'll explain—the person I see does not in any way understand where your limiting thoughts are taking her."

Susan began to cry. She took a moment and then admitted, "I am aware every day of my limiting thoughts, but I am so lost in my efforts to do anything constructive about it. I feel hopelessly drained and unhappy."

I responded, "It's as if you are sitting down to take an exam in a subject you have never studied."

"You describe my situation very well," she confirmed.

The story about Susan tells us something very important; we have a tendency to take for granted that we grow and develop as people. As Susan told me after a couple of conversations, she became aware that she had never worked on herself or her limiting thoughts in regard to attaining what she really wanted in life.

The subject I introduced to Susan is personal growth and development. Like all other academic subjects, personal growth is about organizing observations. However, these are not observations related to the world around you, like numbers, letters and objective facts, but your inner world, your sensations and feelings, that need to be organized in a way to help develop the best you.

In the second session with Susan, she asked me why she had never heard of this subject.

"There may be one very obvious reason," I explained. "Many people share this unawareness of their inner life, and rather than pursuing their potential, they live lives of conformity—which often result in uneasiness, stress, chaos, and emptiness. How can you change and accomplish what you want when you're not aware of how your inner life is formed, manifesting in response to how you deal with your potential? To be aware of yourself and know yourself is essential to becoming responsible for your potential. You can change by virtue of the image you hold in your mind."

The Change[8]

As Susan expressed when we discussed the effects of the therapy:

"What has been crucial for my change is this Plus within me. To think of a Plus in me is so revealing; it's not only a point of reference for my thinking, but something I feel obligated to respect and take responsibility for." Susan had a peaceful look in her eyes and her voice was now full of hope and energy. "It's something I have to take care of and nurture, like the tree you told me about. I understand now that my Plus is something I have to take advantage of… before all of this understanding, I was completely unaware."

Responsibility

For a long time, Susan had been frustrated, with what she considered to be uneasiness and depressive anxiety. She had been prescribed medications by her doctor for the last two years, making her mood flat and unfamiliar. She was unhappy using medications, but had no idea how else to deal with her unwanted emotional state.

The anxiety, depression, and stress in Susan's life appeared to her in quite a different light when she was presented with the analogy of the tree. The tree analogy resonated well. The seed of the tree constituted a blueprint of everything the tree could represent or become, with some possibilities perhaps twice or even three times as grand and beautiful.

When we look at ourselves in light of such a blueprint within every cell in our body and mind, many people get a new view of their pain. Susan, like many others, did not know how big her need was for an alternative way of looking at herself. Very few are accustomed to the idea that you actually take responsibility for yourself when you see your suffering in the light of your best, and our capabilities as a whole human being. Rather, we tend to come from the philosophy that responsibility is to work hard and suffer sweat and tears.

Curiosity

For you to be aware of the things you are capable of as a whole person, your conscious thoughts and language must be in alignment with your Plus. Very often, however, we are not kind to ourselves—more often than not, we beat ourselves up, which can completely block us from becoming enlightened by our potential. Consequently, we may walk through life, as Susan had been doing, with an unknown personal potential that exists alongside low levels of self-confidence, and many academic degrees.

Curiosity is the key when you are trying to become aware of your personal potential. If there are any contexts you fail to understand, i.e., how you are as a person, and how people respond to you, then it's important to stop and reflect about what personal challenge the situation represents for you. Rather, we more often tend to react in our habitual ways and place the reason for our uncertainties or frustrations upon circumstances or other people.

Many of us have been in the same situation as Susan, reacting to our immediate needs, which often are self-centered, and which are powered by habits that repeat our old problems and limitations. Self-reflection in these situations is often equal to admitting our shortcomings, which we tend to do in a self-berating manner, rather than for the purpose of acquiring more insight into ourselves.

These endeavors to know ourselves better are easy to forget, which makes it easy to become irresponsible in regard to developing our personal potential, and look at ourselves in a positive light. So let's take a look at how you can become more curious about what you are capable of representing in your own eyes as well as in the eyes of others, despite the tendency you may have to devalue yourself.

Our everyday emotional and spiritual reality reflects our experiences with the people who are close to us—not just who they are, but how they behave, their interests and personal traits, and their language. For example, the kind of words the people around you use can have a strong influence on your beliefs and your reality.

An illustration of our tendency to be influenced by others is that we tend to like the words that at least three to five people around us prefer. You may have noticed how you use the words or phrases that are expressed by the people around you, and that your thinking is influenced by them, and your emotional reality is shaped by them in certain situations.

For example, many people experience a reality in which they feel their dreams are out of their reach. This is evident in that we are not very good at answering questions about what we desire. Normally when asked about success, people only give two or three responses and sometimes no responses at all.

Many people say they feel locked in their plight, and are not accustomed to a word like "success." Rather, we tend to be locked in a to-do list, and a life governed by necessities. Thus we are more concerned with not being sick, that work is going well, that the kids are fine and that our relationships are okay, that we have more money, perhaps a new car, like our neighbors, to drive to work.

Often, instead of thinking about what we desire, we tend to dwell upon what we don't want to happen – for example, we hope we won't be late for work, that we won't say anything wrong, that we won't forget to lock the door, or turn off the stove—that the things we fear the most will not occur.

It's been said that up to 70% of our daily thoughts revolve around things we do not desire and things that we think we should've, could've, or ought to have done or said. These self-defeating thoughts, motivated by the fear of consequences for our actions or absence of actions fill our daily thinking and limit us.

The higher the percentage of your thoughts that limit you, the less inclined you are to be curious about what you may be capable of as a person, and the more difficult it will be for you to develop the responsibility to make these things happen. This will have disastrous effects upon your life, in a way many people are not aware of, as in the example of Susan.

You have probably heard the phrase "You become what you think." The way your limiting thinking goes, however, is more likely to be seen as a logical consequence of the lack of power within you to view yourself in light of your personal potential. Thus, a more reasonable way of describing the situation is to say "You become what you are enlightened by."

It is common and normal to get distracted by our fears or the negative outcomes we are trying to avoid, when facing adversities in life. While these situations are really opportunities for you to expand your consciousness around what you're able to represent as a person, your lack of curiosity regarding your potential can hinder your personal growth. What you may contribute to yourself and the people close to you may be unknown to you due to a lack of a suitable philosophy of your mind.

The Plus Philosophy

The chances are high that your potential may not be playing a key role in your life, and that you may be unaware of this life challenge. If you are unaware, you risk being hopelessly trapped in your current way of living, unable to establish your goals and understand what your dreams are.

Personal growth and development is a process we experience our entire life; however, most people will not focus on this aspect of themselves until it is absolutely necessary. Not until we encounter some uncomfortable hardship do we make the choice to be curious enough to take responsibility for our own potential, and create a mental outlook that reflects what we represent in our lives.

Susan was curious enough to explore the relationship of her lighter states of mind to her limiting thoughts. She sought help at a time when she felt "Enough is enough!" She acknowledged her situation and understood that she was required by life to change her situation, and she was ready to respond. Susan was eager to take responsibility for her personal potential and launch herself.

When we experience adversities in life, these are opportunities for you to expand your consciousness and become aware of how you prevent yourself by limiting thoughts from pursuing your personal potential. By thinking consistently with reference to your positive potential, like Susan finally did, you agree with yourself that an enlightened state of mind (marked by enthusiasm, passion, and success) is unknown to your limiting thoughts.

Your Plus can be productive when you choose to progress in the blueprint of your best life. Success, enthusiasm, and passion will fill your being once you are able to take responsibility for this hidden part of your potential, or your Plus. Pursuing these light states of mind will help you navigate negative feelings in a constructive way, simply because you have chosen to rely upon the Plus philosophy rather than the defect philosophy. This state of mind is neither on a physiological nor psychological level compatible with uncomfortable feelings and sensations (Holmes, Lang, & Shaw, 2009). It simply fosters development in the direction of your potential.

I believe that it is an inner power within each person to launch the best in himself or herself. Allowing this power to pull you forward when encountering difficult situations, you will answer life and start the journey towards your best, and develop habits and roles that support it. I believe every person is capable of starting this journey and becoming an expert in carrying out his or her potential, and experiencing the positive feelings and empowering thoughts that accompany change in life.

To contact Tom:

www.theplus.eu

www.facebook.com/thepluscode

instagram.com/thepluscode/

tom@plusvendor.com

Sharón Lynn Wyeth

Sharón Lynn Wyeth graduated from the University of Redlands with a Bachelor of Science degree in mathematics at the age of twenty. She began teaching in a public junior high school that same year. During her three years there, she obtained her Master of Arts in education administration with an emphasis in math.

Sharón married an Air Force soldier after her initial teaching assignment, which resulted in her teaching or being a school administrator in four different countries and eight different states, as she was fortunate to always find a job in each location. She retired as a high school principal in 2002, only to become involved with schools again from January 2008 until June 2015.

It was during her time in the schools that she linked the patterns in names to a person's mindset or personality. She worked on figuring out the patterns of the different letters for fifteen years before she fully comprehended all of the nuances. Sharón took the opportunity to travel a large part of the world testing her theories for three years starting in 2002, for she wanted to know if her system was just as accurate in other languages as it was in English. It is!

Sharón is internationally recognized, having helped people from around the world to understand themselves and others better. Her Amazon best-selling book *Know the Name; Know the Person* has received a literary excellence award. She is a frequent guest on both radio and television programs.

What Does Your Name Say About You?

By Sharón Lynn Wyeth

Have you ever wanted to be psychic? The advantages would be that you would already know something about a person when you met them. You would know what modality they used to communicate, what types of gifts they enjoyed, and their style of learning. If you were a salesperson, you could use your psychic abilities to know how to effectively upsell and what was important to them in making a purchase. You could even know why that person was here on earth; what they came to learn, and what they came to share. All of this knowledge would be at your fingertips if you were psychic.

However, you don't have to be psychic to immediately know all of these things about a person when you know how to interpret a name using Neimology® Science. People ask me all of the time if I'm psychic because of the information that I can pull out of a name. My reply is that anyone can learn how to interpret a name. One just needs to be shown the patterns in the placement of the letters and what they mean.

Imagine how your world would improve if, upon meeting someone, you could immediately access information about them? Your communication would improve with fewer misunderstandings. You would not take comments others made as personal because you would be able to discern their motivation and would realize that is just who they are and it's not personal. You could compare two names and see where the potential problems lay and how to prevent them. You would know who is safe to be around and who is not; who to trust and who not to trust. In our instant society, as represented by credit cards and the Internet, we want to have information at our fingertips. Basically, analyzing names, we would understand each other much better and must faster. So, are you ready to read some of the basics of Neimology® Science?

Our first name is the essence of who we are. Our middle name represents how we behave when under stress. Last names represent our environmental influences, which is why people who share the same first name aren't all identical. Said another way, it is as if your first name represents all of the ingredients in your kitchen then the last name indicates the recipes you can make with those ingredients.

So we drop the first name into the second name, adding the middle name for some spice and we get a name reading. Suffices also count, so people who share the same name, yet add additional titles, like Junior, or Senior, or the third, are altering the meaning of their name from someone with an otherwise identical name. That is why people who share the same name in the same family are very much alike and yet quite different.

The first vowel in the first name represents our communication style, our learning style, and the types of gifts we enjoy. The first letter in the first name is the first impression others have when meeting us. The last letter in our first name represents the lasting impression others have of us, and the first thing someone would say behind our backs. The letters in the middle of the name represent those subtler qualities and characteristics that one slowly discovers as they get to know us better.

Vowels represent our emotions while consonants represent our attitudes. We want a variety of vowels in our names as we easily relate to others who share the same vowel in their names, with the exception of not counting the vowel if it is the last letter. The same

The Change[8]

holds true for consonants, as those indicate shared attitudes.

There are two or three ways that the same attitude can be shown in a name with just a slightly different angle. For example, let's compare the first letters in a name of 'J', 'S' and 'W'. One of the qualities in all three letters is the importance of knowledge. However, all three look at knowledge and knowledge acquisition differently.

The 'J' has knowingness. They have what I call 'street smarts.' They just know things. 'J's always have an answer when someone asks them a question and are puzzled that if they know the answer, why didn't the person who asked the question? Knowledge comes to 'J's almost ethereally. It is as if the 'J's simply pull the answer out of the air.

The 'S' represents what I call 'school smart.' They can learn anything once shown how to do it. They want the teacher at their side until the foundation is laid. Then, once 'S' has caught on, they don't want the teacher anywhere nearby. These are people who are smart because of their teachers and/or books that have been read. They are smart due to direct learning. So, 'S's learn from being taught.

The 'W' learns differently still. They learn from experiences. 'W's do not like to make the same mistake twice, and are hard on themselves when they accidentally do repeat their mistakes. Instead, they enjoy making delicious brand new mistakes. The more varied the experiences, the smarter the 'W'. So, 'W's learn from experiences.

Who you sat next to was important in school. You might behave one way if sitting next to a friend and differently if sitting next to someone you didn't like. The letters act the same way. Consonant clusters are formed when two consonants sit next to each other and influence each other in such a way that a brand new quality is created. Let's take the 'C' and 'H' as an example as together 'CH' creates an entire new meaning. 'C' means that the person is charming and charismatic to cover their need to be in charge and in control. 'H' indicates that the person likes to go with the flow. They jump in the river and go wherever the river takes them. 'C' and 'H' are in conflict with each other, as one likes to be in charge and the other enjoys going with the flow. So, the question becomes, what happens when they come together? The person ends up making things harder on himself as he constantly debates when to be in charge and when to go with the flow.

Another example is when the 'S' combines with the 'T' making 'ST'. The 'S' by itself indicates being school smart as indicated above. The 'T' is athletic and needs to be at the top of the heap. If the 'T' doesn't feel that he can work his way to the top, then he refuses to even start. The 'ST' has nothing to do with either of these qualities, as the 'ST' indicates stubbornness and also persistence. 'ST's can persist when most others would have given up; however, they can become most stubborn and get in their own way.

The placement of the letter in the name is also important. Let's take the letter 'M' for an example. Suppose the 'M' is the first letter in the name. 'M' as first letter indicates an ability to manifest in the world their desires. If the 'M' is in the middle of the name, it enhances or amplifies the qualities of the letters sitting on either side of it. As the last letter in the name, 'M' means mischief and hardships.

It took me fifteen years to figure out Neimology® Science, yet it is so simple it can be learned in fifteen hours. My love of names started when I was creating a seating chart for the start of my seventh year of teaching middle school. I realized that I wasn't randomly assigning students to seats; instead, my brain was saying, "Don't put Joshua next to Julie as together they will be clowns, but apart they

The Change[8]

will be okay. Stephanie is going to be stubborn, so put her in a seat where she won't ever need to move. Derek will need extra help, so put him up close." After doing half of my seating charts, it dawned on me that my brain was acting as if I already knew the students. I was embarrassed at first to realize that I was making assumptions about people I hadn't met yet, but then curiosity got the best of me. I wrote down my impressions of each of my one hundred and fifty students using their names and put it aside. I wanted to get to know the students for who they were. I was amazed when December's Winter Break came and I looked at what I had written in September. The accuracy was astounding.

My brain was thoroughly trained in patterns, as I graduated from college with a math major and I have an emphasis in math in my Master's degree. My brain had picked up patterns subconsciously. I wanted to make this conscious.

There was a plethora of Davids in my life. I started by making a chart with multiple columns on it and labeling each column with a different David's name. Inside each column I listed all of the attributes I had observed about each David. Then I compared the lists. What was common to each column had to come from the name David. What wasn't common had to come from the rest of their names.

I made so very many lists over the next fifteen years comparing and contrasting attributes with letters. Once complete, I tested my system in forty-nine of our states and in over seventy countries, as I wanted to know if it worked as well in other languages that also used our same alphabet symbols. To my great relief, it does!

That started over thirty-three years ago. In the fifteen years since the testing was completed, Neimology® Science has grown in its applications. Where once it was only used for seating charts, it expanded to helping people know self better, and improve their relations with others, and it even has the potential to help shy people become more outgoing.

Some Human Resource departments now use Neimology® Science as a strong tool to be used when hiring, as it helps them place the right people in the appropriate jobs so that everyone is happy and successful.

Some lawyers are using it as a hidden tool to help them with more effective presentations before the judges and/or in selecting juries. Salespeople are using Neimology® Science to increase their sales. I'm thrilled at the different ways the work that took so long to create is currently assisting so many others by making their lives easier to enjoy.

Remember, once you know the name, you know all about the person.

To Contact Sharón:

Sharón Lynn Wyeth's Team

www.KnowTheName.com

neimology@gmail.com

210-355-6115

www.BestNameMeanings.com - about names

Facebook - www.facebook.com/neimology

Twitter - www.twitter.com/MeaningsOfNames

LinkedIn - www.LinkedIn.com/SharonWyeth

Mahri Best

I was born in the idyllic village of Uplawmoor in Scotland. I was raised by parents who were incredibly encouraging for me to experience everything I felt passionate about. And so began a life that has taken me in a myriad of directions, and afforded me the opportunity to experience the magic of life.

I came to America at the age of eighteen to be a nanny and have lived here ever since. Witnessing firsthand the lives of leaders, stars, and servants, I quickly grew in understanding of my personal need for honesty and responsibility. It also ignited my curiosity in the successes and failures of mankind.

Throughout my lifetime, I have explored the banking profession, the entertainment world, and the beauty industry – just to name a few. All of these have served as a platform for my life's purpose – human growth potential. Certified as a Success Coach, I'm also passionate about writing, art, and music.

I am married to my soul mate and my best friend, Harry Blum, with whom I celebrate the beauty of life every day in yet another idyllic spot, McCloud, California. I have come full circle and am forever grateful.

Change is Choice

By Mahri Best

Interesting that the title of this book is *The Change*. My take on that title is this: If you are not having the best life ever, change your mind.

Is it a miracle or is it purely a choice? The question, "How is life treating you?" is part of a very old program and needs to be deleted. It infers that the results that you may be experiencing have nothing to do with you. The new and improved program is called, "Giving Choice a Voice."

How does "Giving Choice a Voice" work? This is the talk I've been walking for many years. I've taken every opportunity to put it to the test. There are bounteous examples of how this approach has manifested for me everything I have asked for. And, when I say everything, I mean absolutely everything—good or not so good.

Ask any successful person how they have brought success into their life and I'll take a wager few will say, "I chose it." How do you measure success?

Is success measured by all that you may have acquired in the way of status-related articles? Or is success measured by the peace, joy, and excitement that you exude as you enter the room? Of course, some may say, "Both!" However, what if you are really successful in your life and having all the "stuff" is less important to you than peace of mind?

People accuse me of "being lucky" and while I understand their point of view, I would rather say, "I am fortunate!" I feel fortunate enough to have learned earlier on in the game of life that hidden within every one of life's hard knocks is a huge gift. The gift might not be readily apparent. I have also learned to trust that the gift will always present itself. After all, why would I choose less? Yes! I do believe that I am responsible for everything that shows up in my life. In other words, "there are no accidents." This can be a difficult concept to wrap one's heart around; however, I promise you it is absolutely real. It is with this understanding I began the phrase, "Giving Choice a Voice."

What does this have to do with success in life? It has everything to do with it. One doesn't suddenly wake up one morning and become a doctor or a movie star or a scientist. There is an "inner-knower" inside all of us that will literally jump up and down with joy when shown the appropriate pictures. These pictures might be your creative vision or actual meetings which involve connection to past experience. It is time for us all, as individuals, to pay attention to those signs as we go through life. These signs are not there by accident.

Each one of us comes into this life with a set of life tools, and one of the most important tools is choice. Up until comparatively recently, we have deferred that choice to others who are "older and wiser." I believe that the entry-level being must be given a listening ear. The choices that they are making may, in fact, be the best ones for them in relation to their journey or life experience. What if they really know? What gives us the right to question their ways-of-being?

Seldom do we ever involve ways-of-being as a guide or register of success. When I discovered the truth about creation and my responsibility to that, it opened up a whole new world for me. What that meant to me is that I am responsible for all that is showing up

The Change[8]

in my life. Nothing happens without my invitation. Oh no! How can that be? This can feel daunting to some, yet to me it has, in fact, brought more peace of mind. Hear me out. So long as I am at this tiller of this ship called "Life," I will make sure I follow the path that I know will bring the very best for me and for all those taking part in this sequence of life.

What is the main ingredient? Intuition! Yes! You heard me: intuition. We were all born with instinct. It is a natural part of our being. Throughout life we have all been guilty of ignoring our instincts. And in hindsight we play a mean game of should have, could have, and would have—to no avail.

Oh! I had my story of should have, could have, would have. I have so often wondered how different my life would have been had I paid attention to my intuition in that split second of choice.

The year was 1964. I was a nanny to the four children of an orthopedic surgeon and his artist wife in Rockville, Maryland. It was my day off, and another nanny and I decided to go and explore the nation's capital, Washington, D. C.

We took a bus into town, and it took us past the White House and deposited us at the corner of Pennsylvania Avenue and 15th Street, N.W. where there was a drug store. It was the old-fashioned kind, with a counter where you could sit and order sodas, coffee, and a bite to eat.

While we were seated there, a gentleman sat down next to me. As he overheard me and my Scottish nanny friend chattering away with our broad Scottish accents, he asked where we were from. He was extremely well-dressed and very courteous. We both felt totally at ease talking to him.

While we were talking, he asked me what I would really like to be. Clearly, he thought being a nanny was only a way for me to be in the United States. He was right. I told him I wanted to be a singer. He said, "So, sing for me." And without hesitation, I launched forth into my rendition of "Tammy"! I sang it with all the gusto I had, and everyone at the counter applauded. I had no sense of nervousness. I felt totally comfortable.

The gentleman then asked, "What are you girls going to do today?"

"We're going to do some sightseeing!" I answered.

"Well! I have a car and a driver, and I would be delighted to take you wherever you choose to go!" My friend and I looked at each other. We couldn't believe how nice this gentleman was being. "Thank you!" I said, "That is really kind of you."

We spent the entire day traveling in his limousine, stopping at the Lincoln Memorial, the Washington Monument, Arlington Cemetery to visit the grave of John F. Kennedy, and so many other sights. All the while, he asked me to sing for him. I loved every minute of it. Someone other than myself liked what they heard in my voice.

It was getting dark when we arrived at the office of his attorney friend in Washington. We walked into that office, and I remember thinking it was so posh. It was like something I'd seen only in the movies. Our new friend turned to me and said, "I'd like you to listen in on this conversation I'm going to have. Pick up that extension when I motion to you." He dialed the phone and then motioned to me to pick up the extension.

I heard the voice on the other end answer, "The Living Room." He said, "Yes, I'd like to speak to Mr. Sinatra please. Tell him it is Rod here."

"He's not here yet, Mr. Eh?"

The Change[8]

"Steiger, Mr. Steiger!" he said. "Please give Mr. Sinatra a message from me. I have a young singer I wish to introduce to him. He really needs to hear her. I'll be in New York next week and I'll be sure to let him hear her sing. Meanwhile, he can reach me..." As I listened, I was totally dumbfounded. I felt huge excitement and total trust in this man.

Mr. Steiger was a perfect gentleman. He made sure his driver took us back to Rockville. When we reached the subdivision where we were living, we thanked the driver and got out. I had been thinking all the way home about how I would tell the parents of my charges about our escapade. Of course, I had given Mr. Steiger my phone number, or rather my boss's number, so that he could reach me.

Mr. Steiger had told us who he was and identified himself as having played Al Capone in the movie of the same name. I had never even seen the movie and had been a little embarrassed about that. There was, however, no doubt at all he was who he said he was. However, my employers felt differently. They sat me down and told me that they had not given me the phone when Mr. Steiger called, as they had no idea who this man was, and they were responsible for me here in this country. I felt totally humiliated.

Looking back on all of this, I have absolutely no surprise or feelings of resentment toward my employer. At the time, I was totally furious with them for not letting me speak to him when he called. Did I let them know that? No, because I had been taught to always be polite to my elders. They did what they felt best. They were responsible for me as their 18 year-old nanny all the way from Scotland. Also, I had a contract with them as a nanny for one year and that year had only just begun.

How would my life have been different? Let me count the ways. Am I sorry? Absolutely not! Everything happens as it is supposed to. Of that, I am absolutely sure. What did I take away from this as a lesson? I learned to be more willing to stand up for myself and understand the perfection in everything. There were still many more lessons I would have the opportunity to experience during my tenure with these employers.

We all have stories like these that tell of our near misses. That huge fish we almost caught, that car we almost won. No, there is no doubt in my mind that when we begin to take responsibility for our lives and accept the disappointments along with the victories, we will all experience the magic of life. It is all about choice.

One night in 2001, I was awakened from a dream where I had been shown an interesting concept involving teaching people how to pay attention to their intuition.

By this time in my life, I had finally resolved that those Guides or Angels that had been showing up in my dreams and in my waking now, too, were there for all great reasons. I even asked them if they had names and, without a moment of hesitation, I heard Aesophocles and Andante. I knew, intuitively, which one was which. Aesophocles was the plodder and thinker, and Andante was the fun-like spirit.

Together, they guided me to design a workshop entitled "That Little Feeling Workshop" (TLFW). The positive outcome experienced, as a result of this experiential workshop, owes all of its success to the connection of feeling with intuition and chosen ways-of-being. The TLFW was originally designed primarily for children ages four through ten years old. I soon discovered, however, that the parents were experiencing great benefits from the program. How did this come about? The parents learned from the children.

I'm totally aware that the "old ways" of dealing with life situations are just that—*old* ways. We must begin to think of ourselves as human computers. Each one of us has some "old program" or belief

The Change[8]

that needs to be deleted. Nature abhors a vacuum. Therefore, it is necessary to install new updated programs and then teach ourselves how to utilize these programs in the most effective ways to align with the now.

Begin to think of life as a game or an ever-unwinding story that serves us in the most efficient and rewarding ways. The new plan for life that shows progress is the plan that creates a win-win. Instead, of setting each other up in competition, or a better-than dialogue, let's set out for a win-win. Our willingness to share our wealth of knowledge and understanding is only aimed at a win-win.

Clearly, we all bring to the table different attributes. Those different attributes are not about being better than. The attributes are there as a tool for sharing, as teachers, with those who feel they are passionate about learning more.

Being a product of the '50s and '60s, I personally felt boxed in with labels. When it came to the structuring of our classes and even classrooms, the stigma that went along with the numbering of the students, classes, and classrooms brought focus to the level of understanding or misunderstanding of each student. This focus had only two ways to go. One was to be admired and the other was to be reproached or judged in unkind ways. Therefore, instead of feeling a part of the learning process, one was either set up to hold the elevated spot or to forever feel shadowed or less than.

As I have earlier stated, we now have an opportunity to create a new and improved pathway; one that nurtures those subjects identified with passion from within our 'being-ness.' We can begin to excel in those avenues of our lives that bring us passion and most of all, hopefulness and a greater self-esteem. We can begin to become excited and satiated by our healthy involvement in our own forward progress.

The other exciting component I discovered while exploring TLFW is the musical attribute. Our bodies are made up of a minimum of eight Chakras. Chakra, in Hindu tradition, is an energy point or node in the subtle body. Chakras are part of the subtle body, not the physical body, and as such are the meeting points of the subtle (non-physical) energy channels called Nadis. Nadis are channels in the subtle body through which the life force (non-physical) or vital energy (non-physical) moves—or channels for the flow of consciousness (Wikipedia).

Each Chakra carries with it color and musical sound. By creating a mantra (a feel- good statement), e.g. "When I sing I feel joy in my heart," and by identifying those key words of the mantra, we can then put color and music to this personal mantra.

Note Chakra Name Definition Color

C 8th Aura Connection to the next plane White

B 7th Crown Divine Wisdom   White

A 6th Third Eye Intuition Violet

G 5th Throat Communication Blue

F 4th Heart Love/Compassion   Green

E 3rd Solar Plexus Personal Power Yellow

D 2nd Sacral Sexuality/Relationships Orange

C 1st Root Grounding Red

For example: Let's say that those key words from this example are: Sing, feel joy, and heart. In identifying where, within the Chakras,

The Change[8]

the sound of these words resonate, we begin to understand the correlation as we connect the definition.

Sing might resonate in the throat G

Feel may resonate in the heart F

Joy might be felt in the crown B

Heart might resonate in the heart F

When these notes are sounded together, the recipient feels a connection that only they can describe and often that connection brings a peaceful experience.

Understanding what brings us to our individual place of peace is so important. There are so many choices we can make. As soon as we realize that life is absolutely what we make it, every choice we make is yet one more notch in our belt of life.

I have learned the power of living life in this moment. Any time spent wallowing in the past or worrying about the future is total nonsense. We were given choice for a reason. That reason is for our own good and nothing more or less.

This is why I say that the sooner we recognize the power in ownership of choice in this world, the sooner we will experience the peace that we all say we desire.

"Change is Choice" is the title of this chapter, and I'd like to leave you with one more thought. If you can visualize something wonderful for yourself, and even allow yourself to feel the excitement of that visualization, it is a done deal.

My husband and I recently had a discussion about what we would love to have in a future home. We discussed all the various possibilities and came up with a list of 30 items. Every item we had agreed upon.

Shortly after we made up this list, we were driving through a little town called McCloud, California. We were drawn to this charming little house that, incidentally, had a for sale sign in front of it. We immediately called the listing agent and made an appointment to see the house.

It was love at first sight. And it had everything but two of the items on our list. We decided that those two items would not preclude the buying of our home. Two days after we moved in, a couple of friends of ours from L. A. stopped by to see us. We mentioned that we had made a list and only two items had not been included.

"Oh! What were they?" the wife asked out of curiosity.

"A sauna and a truck for Harry," I answered.

Later that night they called us to say, "We would like to buy you a sauna as a house warming gift." I then just happened to look up on a kitchen shelf and there sat a model of an old Ford truck. The previous owners had left the truck there. The lesson: Be clear in describing what you want in detail!

Remember, there are only three things to do in order to achieve all that you desire:

    1) Ask

    2) Believe and

    3) Allow.

Change your life to be what you desire. This is your choice.

To Contact Mahri:

mahribest@gmail.com

MahriBest.com

Diana Allen

Diana Allen has, for the last twenty-eight years, been a shaman, musician, and artist. During this period she has pioneered the synthesis of traditional and other compatible healing modalities. In 1994, she left Canada and began a transformational journey. She has lived at many sacred sites, studying and teaching in twenty-five countries on six continents.

Diana has created a holistic, integrative, powerful method to assist her clients in releasing limiting patterns held in their cellular memory. This leads them to greater freedom, less stress, and a more intimate relationship with their bodies.

Your body has an innate wisdom to move beyond old conditioning and to heal chronic pain and disease. Diana teaches and coaches those who seek to experience their lives with greater purpose, vision, joy, and gratitude. She uses various techniques in private sessions, webinars, and the written word, to inspire her clients.

Diana continues to tap into ancient wisdom, as well as mysteries held within the earth. She sings these wisdoms through transcendental vibrations. She also plays soul-songs on the piano, and paints soul-portraits of people's energies.

Be Your Own Healer

By Diana Allen

This is your invitation to learn to take full responsibility for your own health and well-being. You will be shown a process that allows you to accomplish this, while at the same time supporting you in becoming your own healer. I will provide you with simple and powerful techniques that will show you how to access your body's own innate wisdom and reclaim sovereignty over your very being.

In 1987, I woke up. While attending The Pursuit of Excellence, the persona I had shown to the world began to shatter. I had attended many seminars and workshops for fun, yet I had never learned to look inward. My typical way of operating was hiding out, feeling disempowered, and believing I was a background person. The first evening, the facilitator confronted me.

Speaking into the microphone in front of three hundred people, scared to death, I hid behind humor, as was my custom. She interrupted me and asked, "What is it that you want?" I made my request and as I was taking off my nametag, she said, "If you don't ask for what you really want in your life, how do you ever expect you will ever get it?" My immediate thought was, "Who is this bitch telling me how to live my life?"

During a break on Saturday, she came up to me and said, "I get mixed messages from you; on one hand I see a confident person, but I also see another person." Without another word, she walked away, leaving me reeling from the punch. She had seen a part of me that was unaware of my true self. My cover had been blown apart, revealing the empty disconnected way I had always felt.

At this time, I still had no idea of the unresolved shock and trauma from an abusive adopted mother that was held in my physical and emotional bodies. My symptoms included a back injury, gastritis, anxiety, and depression. Due to the abuse I experienced, I retained only five memories of my childhood prior to the age of thirteen.

By the end of this two-and-a-half-day program, I knew there was no turning back, and signed up for a five-day intensive. At the end of the program, she said, to me "You have a lot of good things in there; you just need to find them." She had thrown me a lifeline, and I had caught it. From that moment forward, I began a transformational healing journey at warp speed.

One of the most important concepts I learned in the Pursuit of Excellence was to become more aware of my communication. For forty-two years, I had been unaware of the way I spoke. I had operated on automatic pilot, rarely listening to or hearing what I was saying. Now, the powerful lesson was to speak in the first person and become accountable for my self-expression.

A great many people say "you" when they are speaking about themselves. When this happens, I experience momentary confusion. Are they are speaking about themselves or about me?

Another common example is a generous sprinkling of "you know," "like," or "um" in conversations. Often people are unaware of this speech pattern. Nor are they mindful of the price they are paying, which is the absence of clear communication, and clear communication has a profound impact on every area of life.

> "With Diana's teachings I have discovered that my communication with others has never been entirely clear and I haven't always had the confidence to be open and honest. She is helping me to change all of that and it is having a profound effect on all my relationships. Diana is the most wonderful person to work with. I know I can put my utmost trust in her with every aspect of my life." *A.M.Y., England*

Here is another example. I was watching *Dancing With The Stars*, and, one dancer had sprained his ankle. He said, "We sprained our ankle and all last week we had to wear a boot." Who is the "we" he was talking about? Was he connected to his body, or was he ignoring a warning not to dance beyond his level of fitness? The consequence of not paying attention was his sprained ankle.

When a change in the level of your awareness is required, guidance will be available. You may, however, have to take action to access that guidance. It usually begins as a gentle tap on the shoulder, and when you respond appropriately, that is enough.

If you persistently ignore the gentle messages, you can expect an increase in volume, urgency, and intensity. The extremes may be experienced as a serious illness or injury.

A common example is a person who chooses an abusive relationship time after time, then denies having made the choices. Same drama, different face.

Only when taking responsibility for experiences and communicating them clearly can you create a life by conscious design, and expand your awareness. The alternative is to continue to live as you have been. For permanent changes to occur, you must connect with the healer within. This requires a conscious connection to the infinite source of being.

In my own life, I experienced this as the pull of my soul demanding I change, evolve, and awaken. From that moment forward, my life took on a whole new meaning. Getting caught up in the challenges of daily life can prevent us from remembering our connection to our source.

Western propaganda uses war-like images: "fighting cancer," "war on drugs," and "the war on terror." When you ignore feedback from your bodies, or fight them, unresolved issues appear emotionally as rage, blame, frustration, resentment, or depression. In the physical body, arthritis, cancer, heart disease, and joint injuries could be viewed as red flags.

Often people take painkillers to block their symptoms. Rather than seeking the benefit of their own body wisdom, they stifle their body's wisdom with medication.

Acknowledging repressed pain is the first step in understanding that these messages have transformative power. This recognition can lead you out of denial, distraction, and head-in-the-sand behavior and toward becoming your own healer.

Limiting beliefs tell you to look outside of yourself for answers, and give someone else authority over your choices. Have you given away your right to choose what is best for your health? Your body? Your life? Are you masking core issues with band-aid techniques or pharmaceuticals instead of real healing?

In the following article, "American Addict: The Medical Police State," Jon Rappoport points to an approach that has become our first response:

> "The addiction to medical drugs is fueled by the invention of a disease-label for every conceivable behaviour and human reaction under the sun. Here is the dependency formula: I

need to rely on others to understand myself; I need to listen to the advice of friends and family; I need to listen to the experts; I need to belong to the group; I need to think as the group thinks; we all need to wear our disease-and-disorder diagnoses as badges of pride and honour." *www.nomorefakenews.com July 22, 2015*

Accessing Body Wisdom

The following simple yet powerful techniques will support you in accessing your innate healing abilities. They will empower you to make conscious choices for your well-being. You have multiple bodies: spiritual, physical, mental, emotional, and intuitive. These techniques will allow you to communicate consciously with all your bodies, and to use the physical body for feedback. Here the word 'body' will refer to all of these bodies.

When you begin to have conversations with your body, you may be surprised at how willing it is to share its wisdom. Perhaps you have ignored and undervalued it for many years, and it will be delighted that you are finally paying attention. It is important that you ask clear, concise questions. Ask one question at a time, and only questions that can be answered with "yes" or "no."

When you are ready to begin, stand with your feet approximately six inches apart, knees slightly bent, and say, "Body, I would like to access your wisdom." Your body will move in one direction for "yes" and another for "no." The movement is independent of conscious thought, since your body responds energetically to your request. Resist any temptation to prejudge what these movements will be.

Trust your body. Practice until you are comfortable accessing your body's wisdom with consistent "yes" and "no" responses.

First say, "Body, please show me which way is 'yes'." Once you are satisfied with your response to the "yes" movement, say, "Thank you, body. Now, please show me which way is 'no'." Allow the energy to move you. Again say, "Thank you, body."

This method can be used to gauge your body's response to medication, food and drink, exercise, or what have you. Simply ask, "Does this contribute to my vibrant health, now?"

You can also ask your body what clothes it would like to wear by touching each garment and asking the question, "Body, what would you like to wear today to look dazzling?" When I ask my body if it would like a croissant—I live in France—sometimes the answer is "yes" and sometimes "no." If the response is "no," I have the option to listen or not. Making this choice has consequences.

When you look in the mirror, you have options. One is to say, "Body, you are looking great today." Another is take a self-critical approach and say, "You are so fat and ugly." Is it time to show more love, gratitude, and caring towards your body? Acknowledgement that your body is your creation leads to greater freedom, infinite possibilities, and a willingness to release limiting patterns. If the body you have created is not to your present liking, you can take steps to improve that.

When other people express opinions about what is best for you, ask your body if it agrees with them. If your body agrees, you may want to make some changes, if not, ignore their point of view. You are the ultimate authority on you.

Vibrational Body Alignment

This procedure creates alignment between the physical, mental, emotional, intuitive, and spiritual bodies. The intention is to realign all your bodies to create optimal health. You will experience noticeable results in your physical body.

Evidence that your physical body is out of alignment may include conditions such as one leg being shorter than the other, uneven shoulders, back, hip, or knee pain.

Read the following information first. Then watch the demonstration video at:

www.dianallenshamanichealing.com/the-change-videos.html

This technique integrates Cranial-Sacral Therapy, Chinese Medicine, Acupressure, and Osteopathy; it is safe, simple, effective, and easily learned.

Step One

Ask your body if it is in alignment. If the answer is "no," do the following:

Sit in a chair with your head straight, take three deep breaths through your nose, and allow a wave of relaxation to wash over you. Now say, "Body, we are going to experience a vibrational alignment so we can be as healthy as possible."

Step Two

Behind the bottom of your ears, there is a bony ridge. Place your thumbs on the bottom of the ridge and slowly move them along until you feel an indentation on both sides about half an inch back from the ears. These points stimulate the energy flow in the spine, releasing stress and tension. Focus on your breathing; breathe deeply and slowly, holding the points until the energy begins to flow. Feel the points pulsing, faintly at first, then becoming stronger as the energy channels open up. This may take a few minutes. Hold the points until the pulsing is stronger, and both sides are synchronized.

Step Three

The indentation directly above the bridge of your nose is said to be the third eye. In yoga, this is called the Ajna Chakra and relates to your pineal gland.

Place your thumbs slightly underneath the bone next to the bridge of your nose and under the eyebrows. Create a triangle with both index fingers, resting them gently on your third eye. Hold this position until your thumbs begin to pulse.

In Chinese Medicine, the liver governs eyesight, and the points you have been holding with your thumbs stimulate the liver. One use of this technique is to relieve eyestrain.

Step Four

On either side of your head in the temple area, find the indentation, and gently hold the points with your index fingers. With gentle pressure, move your fingers up on the inhale and down on the exhale until you feel a pulsing. This gentle movement realigns the sphenoid bone, which is a key indicator of alignment.

Step Five

On your left side, place the heel of your left hand with the fingers pointed upwards underneath the ridge described earlier. Steady your head by holding the right palm on your right temple. Move the heel of your left hand up once with a short, quick lift. Repeat on the other side.

Ask your body if it is now in alignment. If not, repeat step five.

Checking your body every morning only takes a few minutes, but it can be a powerful start to your day.

Once you have mastered the physical body techniques, I have also created a method for releasing limiting beliefs that are stored at the cellular level and in the DNA. The following personal account illustrates the value of these techniques.

> "Several years ago, an orthopedic surgeon prescribed that I wear customized orthotics for the rest of my life to address my inability to walk effectively. In October 2014, I experienced my first healing session with Diana in Detroit. I had given up on my life, was walking with a cane, wearing orthotics, and the arch in my foot had collapsed. In the first session, as I began releasing limiting beliefs held in my DNA, a new awareness and understanding emerged.
>
> "Looking after everyone else and not myself caused my body to shut down and had led to a MS diagnosis four years ago. I joined Diana's Be Your Own Healer webinar in December and learned the body alignment technique. I no longer use my cane, am wearing regular shoes free of orthotics, and my arch has returned. Every day, I do the body alignment technique. Also, in three short correcting vision sessions, I have gone from tri-focals to no glasses, except when reading small print in dim light. I am thrilled with my progress and very grateful to Diana." *C.S., Detroit*

We Forget We Remember

While living in San Miguel de Allende, Mexico, I attended a meditation. All of a sudden, I started to sweat, became nauseated, and thought I was going to vomit. I tiptoed quietly from the room down the hall to the bathroom, took some deep breaths, centered myself, and then returned to the meditation.

A few days later while relating this incident to a friend, she said, "That doesn't sound like you. Are you sure that was your energy?" I had forgotten to ask my body at that time. I then inquired, "Did the energy I took into my physical body during the meditation belong to me?" The answer was "no." I cleared my energy field and filled myself with golden light.

A few weeks later in the same meditation group, my throat chakra began to constrict and close. More awake this time, I immediately asked if the energy was mine and the answer was "no," so I coughed and my throat chakra immediately cleared.

Both times, I was reminded how important it is to be aware of and pay attention to what is happening around me.

Here is a technique I use.

"I command and imagine that any and all limiting energies in my physical, mental, emotional, or intuitive bodies that do not belong to me and are not in my highest good be transmuted into the violet light and released. Now! Clear! Clear! Clear! I now imprint new information: I am centered, aligned in love, and fill myself with golden light."

By transmuting limiting energies before releasing them, we are contributing to light and expansion. Releasing anger, sadness, or any other emotion without specific direction adds to whatever negative emotions may already be present.

As a world traveler, I am very aware of how important it is to keep this process in the forefront of my mind, especially in airports. There are all sorts of energies floating around and not all of them are likely to contribute to your highest good.

Grounding and Connection Technique

The following illustrates your aligned connection to both infinite source and the earth.

Do this procedure standing up and ideally barefoot on the earth. Take three deep breaths, and focus your energy in your heart center. Now, imagine a figure eight composed of silver light. The top is connected to infinite source, the bottom to the earth. In the figure eight image, place yourself in the middle where the energy crosses over.

The following is one process composed of the individual action steps listed below. Perform these actions in one continuous motion.

- Place your right hand above your head.

- Imagine your hand is connected to the top of the figure eight.

- Now trace the shape of the figure eight down to your right shoulder.

- Continue down across your heart chakra and down your left leg.

- At the bottom, imagine your hand is connected to the core of the earth

- Now bring your hand up your right leg and across your heart to your left shoulder.

- Finally, bring your hand up above your head to where it began.

- Say, "I give thanks for being powerfully connected, aligned, and focused to both source and the earth."

For a demonstration see the video at:

www.dianallenshamanichealing.com/the-change-videos.html

Greater respect and love for others and ourselves builds trust and opens the door to enhanced appreciation and more fruitful collaboration. This leads to greater fulfillment, sense of purpose, and authenticity. Clearing, aligning, and integrating your energy fields lead to transformational change.

Be Your Own Healer.

Be the Change.

To explore the *Be Your Own Healer* webinar, private sessions, and transformational journeys to France, contact Diana at:

BeYourOwnHealer@mail.com

dianallenshamanichealing.com

Stephanie Chung

Award-winning and internationally recognized Executive Coach, Sales Mentor, and Business Advisor, Coach Stephanie Chung specializes in elite-level executive coaching and high-ticket sales training services. Backed by more than 25 years of leading industry experience, including Team Management, Business Development, and Sales Leadership, Stephanie counsels her clients on proven tactics and strategies that greatly increase effectiveness and substantially accelerate performance.

Stephanie has been credited for coaching and developing some of the nation's most elite sales professionals, and routinely collaborates with notable companies to coach and train sales teams on high-ticket selling. As an authority on all things sales, sales results and sales behavior, Stephanie is regularly sought-after as a Speaker or Contributor for multiple platforms and media.

Based in Dallas, Texas, Stephanie's exclusive services span nationwide with the idea that she can help her clients work smarter, not harder.

One of Stephanie's profound methodologies focuses on developing the supporting teams of high-level executives, particularly with sales leaders. She believes that it is crucial to develop, coach, and utilize the strengths of a team in order to increase top line sales and bottom line profits. By mastering effective leadership skills, business performance will significantly improve through increased productivity and ultimately increased profitability.

Mastering Change: Be Strong, Be Brave!

By Stephanie Chung

Growing up as a military brat, I was forced to find myself very quickly. I, like many military kids, moved around a lot. Every two years, our families were being shipped off to a new base, and though that may sound exciting to some and horrifying to others, it was the only life I knew. It was as if I was given an unlimited supply of fresh starts. I was given the opportunity to present myself to strangers time and time again. Seize new opportunities, new challenges, and new adventures. Yes, being a professional "new" kid forced me to become a change master, which I accredit a lot of my success to.

As a professional new kid I learned to accept and even appreciate change. I understood that change was inevitable, and how I chose to see change would always impact how I experienced the change itself. It could be a good experience or a not so good experience – my choice. The blessing in having a change master mentality is that you look for the lesson in everything. Change isn't easy. Change is hard. Change takes time. However, adapting to change allowed me to experience life anew. Change made me strong and brave!

Now don't get me wrong, constant change didn't come without its share of challenges. Some challenges still linger until this day. Imagine my dilemma every time I have to create a password for my bank account or credit cards. Every financial institution has a series of security questions that seem simple enough to answer. You know the questions: What was the name of your elementary school? What was the street address for the house where you grew up? What was the name of your first grade teacher? Growing up as a professional new kid, I don't have the answers to these questions. I didn't go to one elementary, middle, or high school for that matter. I didn't grow up living in one particular house. I didn't have only one first grade teacher. Yes, I've mastered handling change, but I have yet to come up with an answer for those obscure security questions.

In these next few pages, I'd like to share the lessons I've learned on my road to becoming a change master – a person who embraces change. These seven tips on mastering change are tips that I marinate on often. I hope that you find them helpful. Let's go!

"Excellence is not a skill, it's an attitude." – Ralph Marston

Living on active military bases was unique. It afforded me the chance to see excellence lived out on a daily basis. Imagine living in a community where everyone, and I do mean everyone, was in tip-top physical shape. At the crack of dawn, you'd see platoons going through their morning rituals of running (in perfect formation), chanting, and challenging each other mentally. These star performers had done more by 6 a.m. than most of us had done all day. It was interesting to be surrounded by people who were committed to excellence in all things. Every shirt pressed, pants creased, shoe shined, and hair in place. "Yes Sir, yes Ma'am, thank you Sir, thank you Ma'am," were a normal part of one's vocabulary. There was excellence in action and excellence in speech, every time – all the time. The amazing thing about being surrounded by excellence is that it forces you to step up your own standards. I quickly realized that good was never enough. There's always someone, something, prompting you to do better. If everyone in your sphere of influence is really good, how, then, do you stand out? By being stronger, faster, better – by being excellent.

The Change[8]

It's ironic that soldiers act, think, dress, and train in uniformity all for the sake of one day being able to fully function in the midst of complete, dangerous chaos. This is change mastery at its finest.

Complete chaos is often how we civilians feel when thrown into a change situation. However, like these brave men and women, we must prepare for change before it actually happens. Mentally, physically, and attitudinally, we must be prepared.

"I may not be perfect but parts of me are pretty awesome." – Ashleigh Brilliant

As you can imagine, growing up as a professional new kid committed to excellence, I consistently stuck out. I didn't look like other kids, and depending on the region, I didn't sound like other kids. However, never fitting in was a blessing in disguise. I had to work extra hard to relate to people, to befriend people, and ultimately to understand people. And not just understand them on a macro level, but also truly understand them and the essence of who they were on a micro level. That childhood awkwardness of intently understanding people was God's way of preparing me for what was to come. Little did I know that He would use that gift of exhortation to impact my world and those around me. To this day, I feel more comfortable standing out than trying to fit in.

The truth is, none of us were ever created to fit in – we were created to stand out. Stand out in our uniqueness, gifts, talents, and purpose. We often melt our essence to harmonize. The trade of forfeiting yourself to be accepted by others only makes you unrecognizable.

Confidence in accepting one's uniqueness is essential when mastering change. Being grounded in who you are and what you're capable of allows you to put all of your focus on properly navigating the change ahead. You are allowed the privilege to think on your own and ride without the training wheels.

"Say what you mean, mean what you say."- Lewis Carrol

When change is taking place, communication is pivotal or else change won't happen. However, not all communication is equal. There is good communication and bad communication. We've all seen the movies where a solider is standing at attention and his lieutenant is in his face screaming something obnoxious. That may work in the military, but definitely nowhere else. When in the middle of navigating a change, choose to use straightforward language. This is the clearest form of communication. When leading others, I become laser focused on how I communicate – my listening skills heighten and my questioning techniques elevate. I respect that words have power; they are not for eating, so I do not sugarcoat. I do not give excuses, and I do not accept excuses; I only focus on results. Excuses take away your credibility. You can spend time explaining why it didn't work or you can spend time figuring out how to make it work. Time is the most valuable currency, so I prefer to spend it wisely.

Likewise, being clear with one's communication does not mean that you can be disrespectful with your communication – there is a difference. And since communication involves talking and listening, it's imperative that you treat people with dignity. That means give them your undivided attention when they're speaking. In todays' multitask society, giving someone 100% of your attention is easier said than done. However, it is doable and it is necessary. The best way to do that is to listen to them intently, not with judgment, but with openness – openness to better understand their perspective. Whether or not you agree with their perspective is a moot point. Effective communication is simply acknowledging that I hear you, I see you, and I understand.

"Get up! Get Focused. Fight." – Me

The Change[8]

A million thoughts fluttered through my mind as I tried to comprehend one word—Cancer. Who knew that a short, six-letter word could change your entire life? In 2008, I was diagnosed with breast cancer, and my life shifted into perspective. It is an ugly disease that opened my eyes to a beautiful life. Cancer made me strong, cancer made me unbreakable, cancer made me a survivor.

An interesting thing happens when you are in the fight of your life. All of what you're made of comes to the surface. Your fears, your faith, and your grit all come bubbling out – the military mindset that was embedded in me, the upbringing which led me to a no excuse mentality, the professional new kid that always stood up to change – all were vital resources. This was my biggest change to master and I was going to need everything that I had mentally, physically, emotionally, and spiritually to win this battle. Completing this mission was a must!

Beating up cancer reminded me that every breath you take is a blessing and that we must appreciate all we have. Instead of seeing the negative, transfer it to a positive. It could always be worse, so appreciate the little things in life instead of just the big.

- Every 3.6 seconds, someone dies from starvation
- More than 1 billion people do not have access to clean water
- There are 100 million people who are homeless
- More than 2.8 billion people live on less than the equivalent of $2 per day

Whenever I feel upset or angry, I read over these facts, and it reminds me to keep things in perspective. Gratitude has benefits beyond the obvious. According to *Forbes*, "Gratitude improves relationships, physical health, psychological health, sleep and self-esteem."

We all exist, but what you do with your life dictates if you're living. Are you pushing yourself? Are you tasting the fullness of life? Do you need to get out and explore the world, laugh harder, smile more, and immerse yourself in the precious moments? It is about creating your own space in this world. It is about being who you are. It is about realizing and discovering the true secrets to life and happiness. All the dreams wandering around in your head – fulfill them. All those fears – suppress them and take the risk. Life is one big journey, but ask yourself, "Am I living? Or do I just exist?"

When mastering change, sometimes we must resist the urge to flee. During my cancer fight, there were times that I literally wanted to crawl into the fetal position and cry. The changes my body, mind, and spirit were going through were gut wrenching. Mastering this particular change was challenging, and it required much more of me – I had to get up, get focused, and fight!

"Sometimes you have to embrace the SUCK." – Navy Seals

My life took a turn and pushed me down a new path, which then allowed me to stumble upon my purpose. Our company got bought out and I knew my time was limited, but that didn't ease the pain. As they were laying me off, it felt as if they were reading the eulogy of my confidence. Beyond my ego being bruised, it went deeper – I felt the ultimate betrayal. I had spent 14 years with this company, played a pivotal role in the progression of the company, and stuck by its side despite more luxurious offers, because to me, it was family. I was upset, I was confused, I was angry, and I was overwhelmed with emotions. It felt as if I was pushed down a sinkhole and rock bottom caught my fall. On November 11th, I left the office and closed that chapter of my life.

Now, the thing I love about rock bottom is that it gives you a new perspective, a new view, a new outlook. J. K. Rowling once said,

The Change[8]

"Rock Bottom became the solid foundation on which I built my life."

I spent some time crying, and letting my emotions break free. I allowed myself a week to get it all out of my system, but after that, it was time to move on. I could spend more time sulking in my pain, but what would that do? Life goes on whether or not you are ready. It is the one train you cannot afford to miss. I needed to move on. You see, "Pain is inevitable, suffering is optional."

Pain is something we all have to go through. Pain is a part of life. Pain is what molds us. Pain is a teacher. Yet, suffering is our choice. Suffering is allowing yourself to dwell in pain. Suffering is taking advantage of the victim role. Suffering is letting the pain control you. You can let go of the pain, transform the pain into motivation, and learn from it. But suffering is not an option if you are seeking success on mastering change.

I decided I was not going to let this situation define me. I looked up to see the beauty of a new beginning, a fresh start. It was as if I was a professional new kid again and the possibilities were endless.

So, I asked myself, "What's next?" I had multiple offers on the table, but took six months to regroup, develop a plan, and refuel. I decided to take a risk and dip my toe into the pool of entrepreneurship. Jim Carrey once said, "You can fail at what you don't want, so you might as well take a chance on doing what you love." And the thing that I loved as an adult is the very same thing I loved as a professional new kid – engaging with people to understand and support them on their way to being their absolute best, continually reminding them that excellence is not a skill, but an attitude.

What looked like a tragic ending to a career actually turned out to be a platform to regroup, reinvent, and revive. Who knew that the layoff would be the birth of my award-winning, internationally known company, Coach Stephanie Chung and Associates? That professional new kid and I now get to do what we do best – coach companies and individuals worldwide on how to become their own change master.

"Be somebody who makes everybody feel like a somebody." – Kid President

No monetary value compares to the smiles and the success stories that I help create. Coaching, to me, is so much more than a job title; it is helping people be their best. And people who are constantly striving for their best are in a constant influx. They too are learning how to become comfortable with the uncomfortable. Enlightening people to see their potential and helping companies develop a productive, successful working environment is extremely rewarding.

As you're going through the change process, be mindful of how people are feeling along the way. Whether you're reorganizing your department, your company, yourself, or your family, it's important to acknowledge the people who are going through the change with you. Change is hard and sometimes people can feel invisible when it is taking place. Be sure to articulate the value they bring to the situation – everybody is somebody.

"Actually, I can." – Nicky Johnston

When wrapping up your round of change, it's time to breathe. You did it. You made it. Great job! Due to the change, you are most likely better, stronger, and wiser than the person you were yesterday.

Success is often the result of an unquenchable thirst for learning. You can learn something from everyone you come in contact with. The more you learn, the more you know – let curiosity become your best friend. Arguably one of the smartest men on earth once said,

"The important thing is to not stop questioning. Curiosity has its own reason for existing." – Albert Einstein

I continue to hit home runs courtesy of the curveballs life pitches. I encourage people to dream big, and realize a speed bump is not the end of the road. Focus. Commit. Achieve. And above all else, laugh at yourself. Have fun. Become a master of change and overflow with gratitude.

I'm cheering you on as you become the change master you were meant to be!

To Contact Stephanie:

Coach Stephanie Chung

469-802-9376

info@coachstephaniechung.com

www.coachstephaniechung.com

www.linkedin/in/coachstephaniechung

twitter.com/CoachStephChung

Nancy Bauser

Nancy is an over forty-three-year severe closed head/brain stem injury survivor. In 1971, she was a twenty-year-old student at the University of Michigan. She was a good student and a sorority president, with a rebellious streak. She describes herself as a hippie who wore clean clothes. Nancy believed that she had her life completely planned out. She was well organized and good at multitasking, long before it became fashionable.

Today, as a Disability Life Coach, Nancy acts as a Trauma Recovery Expert, who specializes in assisting survivors of anything to reintegrate or re-enter an active and interdependent life. Her husband supports and assists her in doing the things that she can no longer do for herself.

Nancy struggles with memory, fatigue, depression, organization, and the high costs of medical care. She thinks of her head injury as the enemy that she has to battle on a daily basis. Her life experiences make her empathetic to survivors and caregivers. That's what makes Nancy Bauser believable and effective.

Nancy credentials include: Nancy Bauser, ACSW, BCETS, BCDT, CPC
Academy of Certified Social Workers

Board Certified Expert in Traumatic Stress

Board Certification in Disability Trauma

Certified Professional Coach

Accept, Survive, & Thrive

By Nancy Bauser

Imagine something that you have trouble doing. That could be anything from riding a two-wheel bicycle, to dancing with a partner, sticking to a diet, or always completing all of your paperwork on time. We all have difficulty doing something or we have trouble being a certain way. That's just life!

Now, I'll tell you my story. It's one that I know better than anyone else, because it's mine. Imagine being somewhere in the Midwest and it's the fall of the year. In the early 1970s, I'm on a serene college campus where leaves are changing from green to red, gold, and brown.

My primary means of transportation is walking. I travel between massive, stately old buildings and more modern construction on my way to classes, the library, or the student union. All I need to do is to fulfill academic requirements and then, my immediate future will nearly be guaranteed. Life is wonderful and I'm very happy!

Then, there is an interruption in my life's plan. It really wasn't an interruption; it was more like an explosion! On November 11, 1971, when I was just twenty years old, I was a passenger in a very small Italian sports car that collided with a very large American vehicle in the Ann Arbor area. In that split second, my career changed from one of a Special Education teacher, to an entry-level position in the field of brain injury recovery.

I got an impressive set of credentials that afternoon. My right wrist was crushed, both my eyes would never again work together and I sustained a severe brain stem injury. Fortunately for me, the driver of the other car was a physician, who immediately began mouth to mouth resuscitation to restore my breathing. I was rushed to University Hospital in Ann Arbor, where I was put on life-support.

I don't remember anything from the following 2½ months. I don't recall the visits from my friends or the daily vigil of my mother, who spent her days talking and reading to my comatose form. Being transferred to the Rehabilitation Institute in Detroit in December is a lost memory for me.

I don't remember anything until February of 1972. My first recollection is waking up in my bedroom at my parent's house and wondering why I wasn't at the University of Michigan, where I knew I was a student. I had scars on my body and a cast on my arm. At that time it was 1972, and in five years it would be 1977. Believe me when I tell you that in 1977, my recovery was nowhere near where it is today. That awareness simply supports my belief that recovery builds on itself. It just happens extremely slowly.

After I completed three months of outpatient therapy, my mother took over. Guided by her own beliefs, she developed a program for me. She took me shopping, where I had to evaluate and make choices about clothing, which she returned afterwards. She took me swimming three times a week, to strengthen my body and to reestablish coordination and sense of balance. My mother's strong orientation for results made me achieve goals. She insisted that I try to do things for myself, so I would develop some degree of self-sufficiency and confidence.

If I tried and failed, then she would assist. She always believed that I could do more and in time I learned to believe that too.

The Change[8]

In 1972, I was concerned with learning to walk without using furniture for support, go up and down stairs, cook my own meals, and set my hair. Things that I unconsciously do today were very difficult and required deliberate efforts.

I could only do one thing at a time. I couldn't eat and carry on a conversation. I used to hesitate between groups of words so often that I was told that I sounded retarded. I didn't like that at all. So, I started listening to how people in the mainstream talked and I copied them. I also had no idea how to interact with others after my injury, so I watched how others did that wherever I went.

Different people who I liked and respected became my role models. My role models changed as my needs changed. I decided to be the kind of person who got treated the way I wanted to be treated. Somehow, I knew that I had to treat others the way that I wanted to be treated.

I had no work experience before my injury. Nobody told me that I couldn't or shouldn't succeed. My job was to go to school and get my diploma. So nine months after my brain injury, I went back to college. I was able to do that, because as a senior in undergraduate school, I was already specializing in my chosen field of interest.

There is nothing magical about me or my story. I've worked very hard for a very long time and I'm still working to maintain the gains that I've made. In 1973, I earned a Bachelor of Science degree in Education. I never pursued teaching credentials because I knew that I just couldn't deal with students, 30 little sources of stimulation that would all be making demands of me at the same time in a classroom. I knew that would be just too overwhelming!

After graduating from the University of Michigan, I got my first competitive job at an employment agency and I was abruptly fired. I was absolutely mortified, because this was the first job that I'd ever lost. The job required skills that I was simply no longer good at performing. I had to do a lot of phone work, which required me to speak, exchange, and record information very quickly. I also had to keep myself well organized and I had to prioritize.

After failing at my first job, I decided to do what I did well. So I decided to go to graduate school, out-of-state, far from the safety of my parent's home. I applied to schools of social work where I wanted to live and that didn't require the Graduate Record Exam (GRE). I did that because since my accident, I was no longer good at taking tests. I was accepted by two schools and I chose to attend the University of Wisconsin-Madison.

Graduate study posed few problems. As long as I could concentrate on one thing at a time, I did fine. Along with my statistics course, I had difficulty establishing and maintaining friendships because I wasn't aware of my own boundaries.

It's pretty peculiar that I could attend a prestigious university and earn a graduate degree, but I couldn't function fully in the mainstream. If a healthcare professional was observing my behavior at this time, that clinician would have to say that I was able to adjust to a regimented study schedule, but not to day-to-day living.

Six months after finishing graduate school, I got my first social work position at a suburban Detroit hospital. Six weeks later, I was laid off. Nine months after that, I got another job and was fired from that one too.

It's important to understand that I could present a very capable and qualified image in a job interview, but I was unable to live up to that on a continuous basis. I just wasn't aware of my deficits and I believed that I was capable of doing anything that I wanted to do.

The Change[8]

From that point in 1977 until the end of 1979, my job expectations and experiences deteriorated. I either quit or got fired from jobs that I didn't like or couldn't do. At the end of 1978, I ran away to another state, where I knew no one. I wanted to start a new life. After only one year, I realized that I couldn't manage my life without help. My injury had become the dominant factor that was controlling my life.

I returned home in early 1980. The first thing I did was to make contact with Michigan Rehabilitation Services. That agency sent a therapist to my house to do vocational, occupational, and psychological therapy for two hours, twice a week. The clinician helped to prepare me for a secretarial position that I held for nearly a year. I absolutely hated the work and got into a disagreement with my boss, who fired me. After exhausting my unemployment benefits, I started a private practice in social work, so that nobody could fire me again!

I felt I could help others to reintegrate into the mainstream, because I was getting pretty good at that myself. The practice was sporadically successful for two very trying years. When my last automobile insurance client terminated, I fell apart and the practice collapsed.

Fourteen years after my injury, it's now 1985; I finally realized that I couldn't do everything that I wanted to do. I became clinically depressed and began to grieve the loss of a life that I could never have. Then another Michigan Rehabilitation Services counselor sent me to a sheltered workshop as an evaluator aide. I stayed there for 3½ very long years, because I could do the job and I was unaware of other opportunities.

The staff changed at the workshop and so did my job responsibilities. I found myself trying to develop the skills that my new responsibilities required. The strain of trying to meet the radically changing requirements at the rate at which they occurred finally took its toll. One morning, I got up for work and the next thing I knew, my boyfriend, who is now my husband, was picking me up off the floor. I'd had my first seizure.

The doctor in the emergency room tended to my wounds and sent me to a neurologist. After experiencing a second trauma, first the brain injury and now a seizure, I was furious at myself. I was angry because once again, I had to find a new way to live and a new place to work.

Given these circumstances, I did what I had done in the past and sought the help of the state. Because the driver of the car in which I was a passenger had no car insurance, I didn't have funds to finance brain injury rehabilitation, because it's so expensive.

In 1989, Michigan Rehabilitation Services sent me to the only brain injury rehab program that I'd ever attended. I really learned a lot. I became aware of the behaviors that could reasonably be expected after a severe brain stem/closed head injury. I also learned that there were things that were beyond my control that contributed to my losing so many jobs.

Today, I'm over sixty-five years old and I'm working in my chosen field of interest, with clearly defined guidelines and goals. I now pay better attention to my strengths and weaknesses. I have been working as a Disability Life Coach since 2011. As a Life Coach, my first responsibility is to connect with survivors of any trauma and break the isolation that so many feel. Then, I ask questions and provide modeling, motivation, and structure.

One lesson I share is that I've learned that I have to accept what I absolutely cannot do, before I will allow myself to begin to learn the skills necessary to do what I want. Then, I must realize that every day and every task is different. Just because I'm able to do something today, at a particular time, doesn't mean that I'll be able to repeat that behavior on another day or at another time.

Remember **trauma, injury, disability, or illness** are the problems. Is it worth the struggle to try to recover? I say, YES it is. I accept myself with all my limitations! I always try to do the best that I can with what I've got.

Making progress is simple, but it certainly isn't easy. It requires commitment and a sustained determination to overcome obstacles and attain goals. My life has taught me that I was not singled out for the terrible misfortunes that I've experienced. That awareness doesn't eliminate or minimize my problems, but it does reduce the suffering that comes from struggling against the unfortunate facts of my life.

I have problems with my memory and making good judgments. I forget lots of things. I will put something somewhere and then just forget where I put it. I miss appointments or I forget to do things that I know that I want to do. I get easily confused and reacting immediately simply cannot be done.

So, what do I do? I know that I need to have a plan. Mine is just three steps: First, it's best to confront rather than avoid the difficulties created by my trauma, injury, disability, or illness. Next, I must think of myself as having a battle with the deficits created by problems. Lastly, as long as I remain ignorant of my difficulties, I will be unable to avoid or reduce my own suffering.

I wish things were different, but they're not. All I can do is the best that I can and like myself in the process. When I familiarize myself with the difficulties that might occur; my distress seems to be reduced, as well as my fear and anxiety about life with all my problems. When I no longer need to be afraid of what might happen,

I'm able to better prepare for the options or Success Strategies that I must use.

In order to make changes, I need to have goals. I recognize my difficulties in the here and now. When creating genuine change, I must make a sustained effort. My experiences have taught me that it takes time and effort to modify behavior. One statement that I often repeat to myself is **Recovery is not only Making Progress, it is Taking just One Step!** I always need to remember that; it doesn't matter where I start, doing anything to make my life better is Making Progress.

In conclusion, I'll explain my Three Secrets to Success:

1) **Recovery is Making Progress.**

It doesn't matter where I start—just attempting to do a little better today than I did yesterday is making progress. Suppose I've been knocked down and I've remained there for an extended period of time. One day, I decide to attempt to lift my body and stand tall. I try and fail, and then fail again. I'm only able to sit up. RATHER THAN SEEING THIS ATTEMPT AS a FAILURE, I see it as succeeding at beginning the process of standing up. Then, I congratulate myself for what I've done and try again later.

2) **Recovery Demands Commitment.**

I need to continually and constantly perform the behaviors that I'm trying to change.

3) **Recovery Needs a Sustained Determination to Overcome Obstacles and Attain Goals.**

When considering obstacles that need to be managed, age must be considered. Whether it's a broken bone, joint replacement, or disease, it becomes harder to heal after injury as we age.

In order to continue to recover and make progress, I need to remember two things:

1) The 4 A's of Recovery: Acknowledge, Admit, Adapt, and Accept

2) I must treat other people the way I want to be treated

These are three additional absolutes that I have to keep in mind:

1) Failure is not an option.

2) I must maintain determination while accepting temporary setbacks. This attitude positions me well for future success.

3) By refusing to surrender to helplessness, I allow myself to accomplish goals and I mobilize my strengths.

Successful people not only have goals, but they have goals that are meaningful for them. They know where they want to go and they enjoy the journey. When someone is moving toward realizing goals that they have identified, difficulties become solvable problems, not insurmountable obstacles.

To Contact Nancy:

Nancy Bauser, ACSW, BCETS, BCDT, CPC

www.survivoracceptance.com

nancy@survivoracceptance.com

Anne K. Uemura, PhD

I've never known what I wanted to be when I grew up. It seems as though I followed the road conventionally (not "less") traveled—university, marriage, a Master's degree, family, teaching Philosophy, a doctoral degree, a professional life as a Clinical Psychologist. Thank goodness that in the last 20 years my path broadened to include the non-traditional. I explored and studied alternative health, past life regression, the Toltecs, hypnosis, healing, and life coaching. Singing, taiko drumming, reading, writing, and being a grandmother of two beautiful granddaughters provide extra riches.

As a senior citizen, I still wondered about what I want to be when I grow up. A theme is emerging: it began when I became curious about the nature of human beings (ethics), was puzzled by how my psychotherapy clients could move past the suffering I saw, then explored the effectiveness of all manner of healing modalities and studied spiritual material to awaken.

Many of us have a question we're seeking the answer for in life. Now I see mine: how do I heal my heart? As I grow older and continue gathering answers for myself, I want to help others with the healing of their hearts. And play with abandon!

Listen to the Cries of Your Heart

By Anne K. Uemura, PhD

Why Listen to the Cries of Your Heart?

When you hear and attend to the cries of your heart, you come to know who you really are. You find what you long for—a loving, holding wisdom to guide you, abiding peace, uplifting joy, your creative potential, and freedom.

I remember the first cry of my heart. I was eight years old and disturbed by what a ten-year-old neighbor boy had done to me in my private parts. Afterwards, feeling dirty, guilty, and confused, I looked up into the Hawaiian sky and asked: "God, where are you?" I needed to know I wasn't bad, that I was okay.

No answer came, but that need for God surfaced as a teenager when I responded to the seductive message of evangelical Christians and accepted Christ as my Savior. For years I appreciated the camaraderie of my Christian friends, but after a while, the Fellowship wasn't enough. Its theology was limited. My soul wasn't satisfied, and I moved on.

I forgot my cry for God for most of my adult life. My days were filled with school, college, a growing family, studying for a doctoral degree, working again full time, and being a single mom. Decades later in my third year of Barbara Brennan Healing School (BBSH), I remembered this cry of the child-me. It was announced that the year would be devoted to our relationship to the Divine. Tears rolled down my cheeks as I remembered my early need to come home to God. How could I have forgotten?

Why "listen"?

I don't believe I am the only one who heard what my heart needed and then became distracted with life. Do you have a similar story? Are your days filled with endless stimuli that bombard your ears?

When you consider, as you might right now, what you listen to— what do all the familiar sounds of your world, your family, workplace, community, and perhaps the talk from TV and radio mean to you?

How about what happens in your mind? Are you in your head, thinking most of the time, reading or mulling over an incident or someone's story? How much time do you spend deeply or genuinely really listening to something or someone with your full attention?

There is a kind of listening that I practice as a psychotherapist or life coach. I attend to what is said at a deeper level. A client may be speaking about how distant her husband is; how angry his neglect has left her. There is more to learn as I listen to my client's needs, pains, and longings; what is being said about chronic struggles and challenges, the patterns and strategies used to cope, the resources and natural wisdom—all of the nuances of an individual's personality.

If you could listen deeply to yourself, can you hear what really matters to you? What are your dreams? What do you truly need?

Why "cries"?

Bring to mind the cries of an upset baby or toddler. The cries are piercing, expressing the pain of having needs denied or ignored. These needs are basic and urgent at this age, and their whole physiology cries out, demanding notice. "I'm hungry!" "It hurts!" "Pay attention!" "I don't like this!"

The unrestrained nature of our early cries changes as we grow up. We learn to quiet our protests. We train ourselves or are trained to delay our need for gratification. Unconsciously, we develop certain defenses, strategies, and beliefs to deaden the pain. In order to protect ourselves from further hurts, we blunt our awareness of our needs and hurts.

Then the cries of the heart are buried by our strategies to counter our early beliefs about "not being enough," "not deserving to be alive," "not entitled to anything." We want to prove that we are of value—we become perfectionists, over-achievers, and people-pleasers. These early wounds propel us to seek hungrily for love in any form—popularity, achieving the best look and body, or giving ourselves away to anyone who notices us. We blunt them with alcohol, drugs, television, food, shopping, and busyness.

If you don't know your heart's cries, make a commitment to spend time with your heart right now.

What "the heart"?

We want to believe we make decisions with our minds. Yet marketing geniuses devote their expertise to get us to buy by appealing to our emotions, to the heart. The heart moves us to act.

The heart, acting like a thermometer through our feelings, informs us of how we are doing. When things are not going well, our hearts are heavy. When there is laughter and play, our hearts feel light. When we experience loss, we are sad. But more, our hearts contain our needs, aspirations, dreams, hopes, and their counterparts of despair, anger, grief, and resistance.

My present focus on the heart aims to balance the strong focus on the mind in self-growth and success training with its emphasis on affirmations and changing beliefs. We are told: change your mind, change how you think, change your beliefs in order to create a different life.

Many find relief by using strategies to attain their goals of the perfect career, perfect partner, perfect family—success. Relief, however, is temporary. Changes inevitably come into the workplace, relationships, and life, circumstances that cause disruptions in what appeared "perfect." People being people bring difficulties into any situation, often triggering the feelings we buried.

It's difficult to use reason to get rid of a feeling, isn't it? It's like trying to convince young children that their fears about a boogeyman or monsters in the dark have no basis in reality. The heart's fears won't be assuaged with words about reality.

What can we do when our mind cannot manage our hearts? This may be frustrating to many, but it's truly a gift. What is the gift? It's not in our best interest to develop cognitive ways to reduce our emotional pain. Our pain serves another purpose: to draw attention to a part of us that needs healing.

An analogy taken from health care may clarify this point. Pain in our body is a signal that something in our body needs attention. If you take the naturopathic approach to a health issue, you will be led to address what isn't working well in your body. Allopathic medicine tends to symptom-manage: find the medication that gets rid of the symptom.

Dealing with the pain without going to the source is only postponing a resolution—a bypass for immediate comfort. Similarly, cognitive methods for emotional or psychological distress can be helpful just as allergy relief medications can be. But such interventions don't change the underlying conditions. They are superficial fixes.

Choosing the Mind as the Authority is Common

I know too well what happens when your mind is your God. I was told in my childhood to rely on my brain because I was told I didn't have the looks or personality to get ahead in life. Since it was my "mom," I paid attention.

Decades later, something happened to wake me up. I picked up *Autobiography of a Yogi* by Paramahansa Yogananda. By the time I finished the book, I realized my intellect had never given me any answers about how to live my life or how to be happy. Whatever it was in my reading—his spirit or the details that shattered my beliefs about what was possible—my life turned 360 degrees.

In the 20 years since that time, my relationship with my heart grew slowly. Happily, I've gained momentum. I've grown more sensitive and gained depth. I am experiencing my young heart—her vulnerability, wounds, her triggers, as well as feeling the prison created by the defenses and strategies used to avoid them. I acknowledged them before, but never felt or lived them. Now I can hear even small cries of my heart—in any disturbance in my peace.

Why listen to the cries of the heart?

At different times in each of our lives, we can hear the cries of our hearts—such as in dramatic life-threatening events such as accidents and health issues like cancer and heart attacks. There are many transitions—from being a child to becoming an adult; getting married or divorced; becoming a single parent; moving from employment to unemployment; slipping from wellness into illness; losing a loved one. Transition events like weddings and funerals are notorious for eliciting family wounds.

We are often told to cope with these passages. "Grief will pass." "What you want will show up." We are encouraged to take a passive role, keep our chin up, and see what life brings. Instead, try seeing these times of disruptions and confusion as opportunities to mine for treasure. It's during transitions that the heart's cries are often heard.

Lawrence LaShan in *Cancer as a Turning Point* has written about women who ignored the cries of their heart until cancer woke them up. I wonder what warnings were ignored before this alarm jolted each into paying attention to self-care.

In my training to become a healer, I was taught that our bodies are the last place where conflicts and disturbance at the mental, emotional, and spiritual levels are registered. When people are awakened by an alarm such as a frightening diagnosis or a heart attack, most attend to the *physical* resolution of the illness. LaShan's work illustrates how necessary it is to attend to more than the physical.

In my life, even though I ignored the cries of my heart, I still responded to my heart's needs in an *unconscious* way. I made choices that were immature and destructive.

Spontaneous Releases of the Heart

I have been surprised at least three times in my life when the cries were spontaneous and dramatic.

At a camp retreat in college one evening, Grace, a senior member, startled me by saying, "You're afraid of people, aren't you?" It didn't take long for images of my personas to come up— relentlessly. I cried at the falseness of each of them all night long. Finally in the morning when there were no more tears, I felt empty, peaceful, and yet new, like a newborn. I didn't know who I was.

Perhaps an unsought spontaneous "enlightenment" experience? It left me peaceful and innocent for weeks.

The second emotional explosion occurred in a group process at BBSH in 2002. I hesitantly indicated that I had an issue to process in front of my over 100 classmates. Nothing that came out of my mouth was scripted or in my conscious awareness. I found myself haltingly talking about the legacy of the Japanese women in my lineage who had obediently taken an invisible silent position in their roles and lives. The pain and agonies of such bondage came into my body and heart, and I cried uncontrollably with great sobs, my body shaking.

After a few minutes, it was over. I was stunned into silence and wonder. I was glad that my heart's burden was lighter. There is more to this story.

(I didn't realize that my heart contained more than just my wounds, but those of my ancestors as well. I learned recently that this possibility has been verified by recent animal studies showing that DNA carries memories from generation to generation.)

The third experience continued the thread about my ancestors. In my exploration of alternative healings, I learned about *ayahuasca* as used by shamans to enter mystical realms. Like others, I wanted mystic visions and experiences.

Strangely though, when the shaman asked us to set our intention for the ceremony, I said "purification." Why did I say that? Yes, I had beautiful images at first, but they were brief. Instead, a long night of purging followed—physical, emotional, and spiritual. After others had transitioned to more usual experiences, I was horrified to realize that I was still stuck in that space.

It was "hell"—absolutely no escape, no rescue, giving up repeatedly, pleading for an end, resignation, acceptance. At first I cried out in agony, I purged, again and again. I danced crazily between willingness and surrender, and grasping for control. The experience persisted quietly but continually until in the early hours of the morning, I was out of it.

During the ceremony, I had received a message from the shaman that it was time to let go of the pain and burden of my lineage. In the near-trance state of *ayahuasca*, I had no idea what he meant. Apparently to reach mystical realms to know Oneness, a shaman guides people through such passages. In the morning de-briefing, he acknowledged my warrior passage and purification. Mostly I felt much relief—I had made it through hell. I also felt at peace and joyful.

I would not choose to cleanse my heart that way again. I'm pleased to know about gentler paths. One such path has integrated my current and past experiences, and my ancestors' agonies. The hell I experienced and the awful pain of being imprisoned came from believing that I can't say "No." I had no *right* to say "No." "No, you can't violate my body." "No, you can't keep hurting me." "No, you can't take away my rights and liberties."

My younger self believed that terrible consequences would come from saying "No." I feared I would lose whatever safety, position, and value I had if I said "No," especially in the bedroom. But recently I found that my young-self had healed sufficiently to be able to say "No" when sex was asked of me. At that moment it was my truth. No fear was there to stop me.

I now realize what a precious moment it was—my personal prison dissolved and perhaps the end of oppression of centuries as well. Beyond the expression and purging of the internal hell created by burying anger, outrage, and despair that I experienced before, my young-self needed this final "No."

When the cries of the heart are not heard

Most times in my life in contrast, the cries of my heart were so muted I wasn't aware of them. Yet they still had power to influence choices that were very hurtful and disrespectful to all involved. The most obvious childhood need was for acceptance and love.

One example that still makes me cringe is when I "abandoned" my children. When I lived in San Francisco after my pre-doctoral internship at UCSF, I was in a relationship with someone who lived in Marin. My need to be with him was so strong that on most weekends, I left my children to fend for themselves at the ages of 10 and 13. Fortunately my daughter "told" on me to my sisters. After I was confronted, I stopped.

Too many of us still make choices from our unconscious, often desperate, needs. Please take the time now to sit and look at your life. Do these stories trigger any memories in your life when you didn't heed the cries of your heart? But rather, you acted out of the cries of your heart in *unconscious* ways?

Because for most of my life I have been deaf to the needs and cries of my heart, I am writing with the hope that you will care about yourself in a deeper way; that you will be curious about what lies at your core to begin to listen.

A Process to Move Forward

What follows is a broad-stroke description of how to deal with the wounds you carry. I will use "two-year-old" to describe the young parts through early years as a toddler, a baby, even an embryo, and refer to "her" for ease of reading.

You start by noticing the cries and appearance of the two-year-old: upset feelings (like anger), defenses ("I don't really feel/see that"), strategies ("accomplishment will bring me what I want"), limiting beliefs ("I'm acceptable only if I'm perfect"). Positive aspects show up in play, laughter, spontaneity, innocence, mischief. Please record each in a journal. Each of these instances can provide you the chance to build a healing relationship with your two-year-old.

For example, if you are angry or find yourself in a defensive mode, you might be aware enough of what is happening and say: "oh, it's the two-year-old." Sometimes acknowledgement of her is enough to ease the emotional grip of a defense or feeling.

The emotions to use for this process are anger/rage and any negative feeling that is an over-reaction, habitually experienced in similar situations, and/or lingers. Feelings are by nature, ephemeral—they arise, are felt, and they pass. If they are overly intense, repetitive, or persistent, they are calling for attention.

When there is time for self-inquiry, select one thing and create the space to fully acknowledge it. Begin the time with yourself by invoking what makes you feel most safe—an experience, a name of something Sacred, some safe connection.

Welcome and thank the young part for showing up.

Accept her as she is. Offer her the companionship and safety that weren't there when the wounding occurred. This is not a place for stories, no thinking, no words, no justifying. Listen. See. Be with.

Be present and be curious, witnessing what unfolds. Relax into the process. (A meditation practice is excellent for building your capacity to be present.)

More Details about this Process

The Change[8]

Noticing is being aware. Carl Jung said "awareness is curative." You can build your self-awareness through different practices. One is to start by deep breathing for a short time. Then, throughout the day, notice when you aren't breathing naturally (when you are tense). As you continue to notice, you will be aware of more. It's the same with your two-year-old. As you notice her, you will see her more often.

You may not feel welcoming or thankful. Think or say it anyway. Your attitudes change in this process.

It's natural to be afraid any time you work with your inner child. She and the adult-you have fears—when feeling alone, insecure, out of control, without power.

When a feeling is overwhelming, return to that place of safety and stillness, your place of respite and peace. You can also connect to a symbol, an object (tree or flower), a song, or movement that brings a sense of safety. Use your imagination to create images for your two-year-old. Send these images expressing love, holding, or security to her. Return to your process when you are ready.

Working with defenses, beliefs or strategies is a bit more complex. After your welcome and thanks, you might ask what more is there. Images, messages, physical sensations, or emotions may come. Be patient. If nothing comes immediately, ask again. You welcome and thank what appears. Witness, accept, and be present to whatever shows up.

The Reward of Going through Your Wounds

This path provides the two-year-old with a corrective experience—giving what was needed at the time of wounding. It attends to the layers of protection around the heart so they can melt away. Gradually, the strategies and limiting beliefs drop away and new ways of being and creative actions become available. The reward of uncovering your undefended heart is experiencing its truth, wisdom, vastness, and Source in Love.

UnearthingYourFreedom.com

SuccessThroughAuthenticity.com

Phone: (707) 337-1883; Skype: anne.uemura14

Jill Kovacovich, RN, BSN, PHN

Jill is a nurse with over 20 year's hospital nursing experience. She also worked as a Public Health Nurse working with families referred by Child Protective Services with children under age five, who were at risk for abuse and neglect. Additionally, she has done outpatient clinic nursing and Home Health Nursing. Currently, she works with the Medicare aged population.

Jill is also a Certified Meridian Stress Assessment Technician and performs saliva bioenergetic testing, which detects functional disturbances early (before clinical symptoms are displayed) and gives opportunities for early change and treatment.

Jill is also an expert on utilizing essential oils for physical and emotional healing. This ties in with her Native American plant-based learning from her Elders. Jill believes, "Plants are God's gift to us and He provided us with the basis for everything we need."

Jill received her Certified Life Mastery Consultant credentials from Mary Morrissey and is licensed to teach multiple Mary Morrissey and Bob Proctor programs. Jill is passionate about helping others live a life they love; turning self-judgment into confidence. EVERYONE deserves to be joyful and free!

Damaged Goods to the Silver Lining

(Unconditional Love)

By Jill Kovacovich

Have you ever been asked to look back at a time in your life that was carefree? When your imagination was all you needed for new possibilities? It is assumed by so many that childhood was a time of happiness, safety, and the freedom to live in a dream world where anything was possible. Motivational speakers use this strategy to take us to a period in our lives before we learned limitations and a self-esteem weakened by the opinions of those around us; and before we assimilated others' opinions as our own. This didn't work for me and even derailed the process.

I was born knowing that I wasn't wanted and I needed to be quiet to be accepted. As a toddler, I learned that I also needed to be invisible to be safe. I felt like I was in the way and was left home frequently. When I was taken, I didn't want to do anything to cause me to be left home alone the next time. I searched to find a place to sit quietly and out of the way, not drawing attention to myself. I had to play in my room when at home.

We often lived in one bedroom apartments, where my room was the couch and a box of clothes next to it. In such an apartment, I was asked to play outside, so my current stepdad and mom could talk alone. I came in two times to ask my mom a question or tell her something and was asked to go outside again. The third time I headed in, my stepdad became angry and grabbed me and put me in a dark bathroom and wedged a chair against the door handle to trap me. I called for my mom and finally to my relief the door opened. It was my stepdad, who grabbed me by my long hair, held my head back and stuffed washrags in my mouth to quiet me. He threatened me with much worse if I caused any disturbance. I sat on the floor in the dark. My mouth felt like it was tearing apart at the corners and it was hard to breathe. A three-year-old mouth is not very big! Finally, the door opened and a blanket was on the couch for me to go to bed. Nothing was ever said about this incident. There were many incidents. Our home was filled with alcohol abuse and violence. I endured every kind of abuse and nothing was ever said.

Fast forward a few years to another stepdad. I thought I liked this one. I'd go on outings and scenic drives with them. I got car sick, but never complained because I wanted to be around my mom. Sometimes, I would lean forward from the back seat and say something to my mom and was told that "kids were supposed to be seen and not heard." Ugh! How many times have we heard that growing up! The scenic drives ended at bars. I sat in the car while they went in for "a beer." Sunshine turned to dusk and then darkness, while I sat in the car. No electronics, books, food, water, or bathroom.

Sometimes, I witnessed parking lot fights and got on the floor of the car, so no one would see me. It was scary, cold, and lonely.

By ninth grade, my mom had been married five times. I was never invited or told in advance of the weddings. As I started a new school year, my mom registered me with a different last name. It was embarrassing because we would line up in alphabetical order and my few friends would be telling me I was in the wrong place in line. I was pretty self-sufficient by then. I had been on my own since the age of seven, when I was paid a dollar a day to babysit myself, buy my food, eat, and have clean clothes. I rode my bike everywhere I

The Change[8]

needed to be. In the winter when it was exceptionally rainy, my mom would leave money for me to take the jitney (which was a small van-like bus) to my appointments. I started taking dance lessons (tap, ballet, jazz, and baton twirling) at age five. I loved it and it was a great babysitter. My mom was a beautician and she paid for lessons with her tips. I got myself to classes and home. I would wear leotards and tights with a jacket over them and ride my bike or take the jitney. I felt comfortable with the jitney driver. He also did laundry and would deliver clean towels to the beauty shop where my mom worked. He was nice and my friend's dad. He would have me sit in the front seat with him. He had cookies or candy bars in the glove box to share with me. He paid attention to me and we talked. One time he parked the van. He said we had to visit awhile as he had driven too fast and could not go back to town until it was time or people would miss the bus. When he was "done" with me, he told me not to tell my mom, as she would not understand and it would be "our little secret." This was not the first time I had heard those words, but it hurt more this time as I had trusted him. I wondered if this was happening to his daughter, also. I never rode the jitney again.

Through the years, I tried to tell my mom about the scary things that happened to me and she responded, "Oh, I can't believe that" or "You must be mistaken." I shut down and never told anyone; who would possibly care or believe me if my own mom didn't? About 30 years later, my mom offered some acknowledgement, but I felt even worse about myself. She said, "I had the same things happen to me and I never told my mother. I would never have considered bothering her with that. She worked hard and had too many things to worry about to be told something like that."

I had many dance recitals, school festivals, and parent teacher conferences my mom didn't attend. She made sure I had the necessary costume, but never showed up. She dropped me off in front of the auditorium and told me to find a ride home. I was a latchkey kid.

Around 4th grade, I discovered that if I did all my work in school and read extra books, the teachers gave positive feedback. I loved the kudos and strived to do better. In high school, I was on the "high honor roll." My mom wasn't impressed by this academic achievement. I thrived on recognition and got involved in activities in high school and college, including the debate team, newspapers, head song leader, cheerleader, service organizations, Homecoming Queen in high school, and First Runner Up Homecoming Queen in college, all while being on the honor roll. The only time my mom acknowledged these activities was when I came home with my Homecoming Queen crown. She took it to the bar to show her friends. These activities helped me feel successful while covering up the truth I knew about me.....that I was really just "damaged goods" and not worth much. Teachers helped me apply for a college scholarship and I got a four-year full scholarship to UCLA. I was so excited, but my boyfriend didn't get accepted, so I didn't go to UCLA. It was too far from home and I didn't want to leave my boyfriend. My mom said, "No one in our family has ever gone to college, so why should you be any different." I got a few small scholarships and a student loan and went to the local college instead. At least I was going to college and I felt good about that.

During college, the violence in our home escalated. I started sleeping lightly and sounds would cause me to be alert and hypervigilant to assess any danger. Over the years, I became adept at separating myself from my body. It was as though I watched myself being abused and only felt pressure. One of my stepdads beat me with a board or whatever he had until I cried. I hated giving him the satisfaction of knowing he made me cry, but it was the only way to make him stop, so I pretended to cry while keeping my head down.

The Change[8]

For years, I watched my mom apply makeup to black eyes and go to work pretending life was great. I also became quite an actress. So good, in fact, that I could even fool myself sometimes! My hair and makeup were always perfect, my clothes were carefully chosen, and I would envision all the possible scenarios I might encounter during the day and rehearse the responses in advance. I was polished, in total control and no one knew me.

If a situation came up that I had not rehearsed, I would freeze inside. The fear of letting people see the "real me" was overwhelming. I never wanted anyone to find out the truth. Once, my boyfriend's mother asked me if that was my mom who was on the front page of the newspaper. I had no idea what she was talking about. I said "no". She was persistent and said "well isn't your mother (name)" and I said "yes". She held the newspaper in front of me and I saw my mom's very damaged car on the front page of the newspaper and quickly skimmed part of the article. I hadn't seen my mom in two days and was actually worried about her as usual. The next day, she had a friend drive her home from the hospital and returned to work as if nothing had happened. She never said a word to me. I knew the article called her a "drunk driver." She started walking to work for "exercise" after that, but never a word.

I married my college sweetheart eleven days after I turned 21, and ten months later we had an adorable baby girl. He attended college during the day and worked in a mill from 3 p.m. to 11 p.m. Just before the birth of our baby, he started going out with the guys from work to "unwind" before coming home. Sometimes he never made it home. He was failing classes and dropped out of school because of drugs and alcohol. I was stunned. This was never a part of the plan. He had been an honor roll student, started working at age 15, and was voted most likely to be a responsible dad driving a station wagon full of kids around. This was totally out of character. We were divorced before our little girl was walking and I was devastated. I felt that I somehow turned him into an alcoholic. I kept trying to figure out what I had done wrong!

As a single mom, I worked 3 jobs to survive. I made sure my baby was fed and had clothing, but I did not eat every day. We had a home, heat, and gas to get me to work, but it was a "no frills" life. I visited my mom one day to discuss my situation and her response was, "I don't want to hear it.....you are just feeling sorry for yourself". I left that day feeling bad for bothering her with my problems.

A few months later, I met my second husband and that relationship lasted over 20 years. What started out as my "knight in shining armor" morphed over the years to a Dr. Jekyll and Mr. Hyde. I stayed married because I did not want to follow in my mom's footsteps of multiple marriages and wanted a stable, intact marriage. I had two more daughters. I couldn't figure out why my husband was always mad at me. One day, I asked him why he was so mad at me. I asked if he was upset with me "because I was alive, took up space, and breathed oxygen." He said "that's pretty much it." Over the next three years, the situation became unbearable and I finally left to avoid teaching my girls to accept bad behavior.

During that marriage, I received my Bachelor's of Science in Nursing. However, feeling the need to prove I was intelligent and valuable, I decided I should get a Master's degree. I received a scholarship to UC Berkeley for a Masters in Public Health. I was very excited. At the time, UC Berkeley was the #2 school in the nation! When I told my husband, he said "over my dead body" and that was the end of it, even though the school offered me married student housing. A few years later, I learned about a Masters in nursing program that I could attend at the local university over a monitor. I was accepted and completed the first year, but dropped out because moving, going through divorce, working and studying proved to be overwhelming. I felt like a failure. My stamina just couldn't keep up with everything I felt I needed to do to show I had value and worthiness.

For the next 15 years, I put all my energy into my children and nursing at the hospital.

My mom mellowed and our relationship started to grow. I found out I had not been wanted and she wished she wasn't pregnant with me. I learned she was married to someone else when she had an affair and I was conceived. I told her that I knew I never had a crib when I was a baby and she asked me how I knew that. I told her I remembered watching her and my dad push two chairs together to make a bed for me. She said there was no way I could remember that because I was too young. She was amazed when I described the apartment, the yard, and the tall stairs on the outside of the building to the door of our apartment. I was careful to not share my feelings from that time because I did not want to hurt her. I also knew I could never tell my story as long as she was living because I did not want to embarrass her or hurt her feelings.

There is a silver lining to my story and it's the most important part of my life! Even though I was shunned by mom's relatives, my paternal grandparents were thrilled to have a granddaughter. My grandma smiled at me, held me gently, kissed me, sang to me, read to me, and I felt safe and valued in her presence. When I got older, we walked together, played games, colored, made cookies (I stirred the batter), picked berries and made turnovers. Later, she taught me to sew and quilt. She took me everywhere she went. The only time I was left alone was during the early morning milking on the farm when it was still dark. If I woke up and she wasn't there, I always knew she and my grandpa were in the barn. She hung my clothes by the fire, so when I got dressed on cold mornings I could put on warm clothes. I didn't have to perform or earn any of the attention or unconditional love. I felt valued and loved just because I was alive. I didn't have to be invisible to be safe. I never wanted to go home and sometimes would hide in the barn loft and hope my mom and stepdad would give up and leave me there.

When I was in 4th grade, my grandpa got very sick and was in the hospital not too far from where I lived. I'd ride my bike to visit him after school every day. He was always so big and strong, I didn't understand what was happening to him. The last time I saw him, he didn't wake up when I went in his room in the hospital and sat by the bed. He just kind of snored and was so sound asleep that I left without getting to talk to him. The next day when I went back, his bed was empty. The nurse told me that "he had moved," but she didn't show me where he moved to so I went home. I remember being confused and sad that I didn't get to see him. A few days later, I was told that he had died and I felt like such a bad granddaughter for not giving him a hug the last day I saw him. I worried so much that he would not know how special I thought he was. He was always busy on the farm, but we still did lots of things together. We would pick apples and he taught me how to hoe the garden and he carved furniture for my dolls. He also convinced my grandma to let us get a pony!

I got to have my grandma for about 14 more wonderful years. She would come and get me every Friday after school and keep me for the weekend. Those visits were life giving. She was consistent in the way she treated me and I always felt safe and valued with her. She was the only person that told me she loved me during my childhood. She planted a seed in me; a seed of love. She consistently nurtured the seedling that sprouted until that love was strong and powerful.

When I was older, I drove to visit with her every day after work. We would visit while eating together. She also showed love to my daughter just as she had done with me. She looked at her like she was an amazing miracle that she was in awe of. She would take her little hand and just hold it and say "God love it."

The Change[8]

One evening, we had an exceptional visit and she held my daughter and cuddled her for a very long time. I went home much later than usual. The next day, my grandma had a massive stroke and I held her in my arms for hours as she passed from this world. The only thing that kept me going was her love. The strength I felt from her love gave me the power to keep putting one foot in front of the other. That was 42 years ago and the love is more powerful now than ever.

I shudder to think where I would be without experiencing such unconditional love. I could easily be an addict on the streets. As humans, we are wired for attachment and I thank God every day that I was given my grandma.

Since then, I've always desired to make a difference in the world. In grammar school, I always said hello to the kids who didn't have friends. In high school, I would sit with students who ate alone. As a mom of young children, I paid close attention to the children whose parents didn't show up to watch them, or didn't have someone pick them up from school. My heart ached for these people because they were "me" at that age. At the time, I didn't understand why I was drawn to these kids, but I understand now that I was sharing and planting a part of the seed of love in me to them.

As an adult, I am drawn to the people who may be highly successful in one or two areas of their lives, but held back in other areas because of the limiting beliefs from their past. My heart aches for these people because they were "me" also.

I felt I had to do something "big" to make a difference in the world. I wanted to make a discovery or invent something that would change people's lives significantly. I now realize my true passion is helping others realize their own power in rising above their circumstances and "history." We all have greatness. It may be a tiny spark, but it is there. I love teaching how to fan that spark into a glowing ember and fanning it more until it erupts into a huge bright flame. The greatest joy I feel is witnessing others come alive in love.

To Contact Jill:

E-mail: jill@jillkovacovich.com or info@jillkovacovich.com

Website: www.jillkovacovich.com

Jorge Aquino

As a personal coach, Jorge specializes in guiding adults and adolescents through addiction recovery, personal, spiritual, and career growth. His work facilitating group sessions for the last five years has focused on recovery-based 12-step programs for Adult and Adolescent Recovery, Adult Relapse prevention, Adversity and Pain.

He specializes in one-on-one coaching work to help adults and teens transform themselves and to learn to courageously access their own natural uniqueness, creativity, brilliance, vulnerabilities, wisdom, and humanity.

With more than 40 years in the hospitality industry, 15 with his own business-planning, coordinating, and catering events, Jorge has synthesized his people skills into a career as a life coach, with the goal of helping people at a deeper level, in order to facilitate sustainable change. Hobbies include travel, cooking, and sports.

Education:

Associate of Arts, Business Administration

Palm Beach Junior College 1976

Occupational Associate Degree – Culinary Arts

Florida Culinary Institute 2002

Occupational Associate Degree- Food and Beverage Management

Florida Culinary Institute 2001

Certifications:

Neuro-Linguistic Programming certification: Steve Jones, PhD, President—American Union of NLP

Affiliations:

Group Facilitator – American Addiction Centers, Singer Island, Florida

The Decision

By Jorge Aquino

My story begins on Tuesday August 16, 1994, a day which unknowingly would change my life from a path of no direction to one fueled by faith with purpose.

A decision which would turn my biggest failure into my greatest strength and change my life as I knew it… forever.

The decision to finally realize my addiction to alcohol and how it had led me to such a low point in my life that I would take two of the most important people in my life—my mother and my son—for granted.

Addiction had created an existence and not a life.

My life revolved around fear, procrastination, plans not fulfilled, dreams left on cocktail napkins, and insecurity about everything, especially my relationships.

My failure only achieved emptiness and purposelessness, leaving me no hope, no desire—just merely existing. It is an existence that many have experienced, but only a few have come back from or risen above.

The lack of faith, lack of values, and the continuation of bad decision making all kept leading me down a dark path, with no perception of a way out.

The Change[8]

Today, I look back and see that the journey has led me to provide value to other people's lives and remain open to all the Universe and my Creator have in store for me. It is a life filled with enthusiasm, optimism, and the hope that I can leave the world a better place.

It is still very humbling for me to know that on August 16th 1994, I burned the boat of my previous life which left me with two options—die an alcoholic death or change and thrive. It left me with the NO TURNING BACK attitude.

I wasn't enthusiastic about embarking on this journey. I kicked, screamed, cried, and entered into all other forms of denial before capitulating. Thankfully, I have been blessed with many wonderful, loving, caring men and women on my journey.

The unconditional love I was shown and the amount of patience, tolerance, and support has been and still is today PRICELESS. For I was not forced to change, but rather suggested that I look at this new way of living without fear, conditions, and other limiting beliefs.

I was allowed to learn, feel, and experience my own spiritual beliefs, removing any preconceived opinions that I had about spirituality. This alone is one of the greatest gifts I've been given. To believe in a spirit and a Universe as kind, loving, and having a sense of humor has been so freeing.

To have the opportunity with this freedom to nurture those relationships of family, childhood friends, and other dear friendships is another PRICELESS gift that is a result of my decision.

Also, the freedom to continue to grow as an independent man, facing challenges I have had in my personal love relationships which involves embracing my part of the failure as well as my successes. Being divorced twice and also having two long-term relationships ending, which in hindsight could have been handled better.

These relationships have taught me to be more present, unplug from distractions. Ask, listen to understand what is being communicated, and how is it being communicated. Be compassionate, show empathy. Don't try to fix, change, or save someone.

These have helped me learn the lessons that led me to live from a place of LOVE in my heart. For I still believe in LOVE.

I have learned to not judge myself too harshly and also not judge others, at all. I have learned that everyone today in the world has a challenge at this very moment. Right now, as you read this, you may have a challenge.

The acknowledgement of non-judgement has led me to have no expectations regarding people, but be more curious of why people behave the way they do.

The expectations that I have for myself are realistic and not overwhelming. They motivated me to succeed and achieve.

I'd like to recognize my son's mother before I move forward in my story. She made a difficult decision to move away. To do so for what she believed was in the best interests of her son, who I see as a person of great integrity. She could not be a better role model for our son. She remarried and with her husband has done such an outstanding, loving job of raising our son as a fine young man, and a thriving college graduate.

My resistance to change is what holds me back at times. It has helped me learn from the consequences of my actions, choices, and behaviors how to be a DAD from 2200 miles away after almost 21 years on this journey.

How does one make a decision to change from a life of despair to a life of love and prosperity? It takes commitment, a word I did not understand before this decision. What I have learned about commitment is that it takes daily effort towards a goal, an accomplishment, or just doing the next right thing.

Doing the right thing now is so natural for me now—no adult supervision needed! Commitment has led me to understand other positive personality traits such as... character, integrity, trustworthiness, honesty, truthfulness, and many more values and virtues that I did not know about and more importantly, did not understand.

Today I know that we all have the potential inside of us and that internal desire to live by these values makes life worth living and not merely to exist.

The joy that comes from being of services to others I now know is my purpose in life—to make a difference in a life today, to add value, to remain teachable. The ability and desire to increase my contribution without worrying or doing so for reward or recognition.

To believe in someone, the way the early travelers on my journey believed in and encouraged me to continue pushing through the tough times; the times when I wanted to quit and give up. The times when I'd ask, yell, or scream "Is this really worth it?"

Change was and has been tough for me and as I have learned, it is more my resistance to change than change itself.

Early on in this journey, the highs and lows would overwhelm me. I would become frustrated and at times question the worth of the decision. The "high" of doing the right thing, being ready and still being turned down for opportunities. When an opportunity falls through, I begin to ask what could I have done differently? What is the lesson that I can take from this experience? This has taught me to live in a state preparedness.

The lows of feeling the loneliness of my son's room empty, after he and his mother had left. That feeling has been the driving force in making changes for the better. That feeling is the reminder at times when I want to give in and quit. That feeling is the consequence of my prior choices and behaviors.

The highs and lows now are a gently rolling highway that I travel, not too high or too low. Just peaceful.

When it comes to financial failures, my decision has guided me to really look at my responsibilities, actions, and behaviors in these lessons.

It really does get easier when one takes full responsibility for ones choices, actions and behaviors. I have stopped playing the victim and have been set free.

Awareness comes from acceptance that the decisions I have made and continue to make are mine. My happiness is up to me and no one else. It is freeing today to know that all of my experiences have prepared me for this moment and the journey ahead.

A journey of awakening for me that involves encouraging, empowering, and inspiring people to let them know it is not too late to follow their dreams. To let them know they can walk to the beat of a different drummer, leave those limiting beliefs behind, and go where there is no path and leave a trail.

As Neale Donald Walsh espouses, "decide, declaring, create and choose who you are and who you want to be." For me, that is a far cry from a life that was full of loss, discouragement, and fear. The only way I knew how to cope was to escape, stuff my feelings, people-please, and wear a mask.

The Change[8]

It is such a great feeling waking up with a purpose, drive, a vision, and goals, as well as love in my heart and mind. When you can become a giver, you can share your gifts for the good of others, and it will transform you.

Being a giver brings responsibility which equal being a model of certain qualities and values on a daily basis. Those values are love, honesty, loyalty, peacefulness, clarity, trust, and respect. One becomes a mentor to others in need and sets an example acting as an inspiration for others who see that if I can do it, they can too.

That is when change happens—when people get energized to make a difference, first on a personal level, then in the lives of others. Today, I have a great opportunity to make a difference and it all started with me and now it is about helping the people around me.

I am especially drawn to help young adults and teens who are just starting out. Sharing my knowledge, mistakes, errors in judgement, success, joys, and triumphs in hope and faith that I can encourage them to embrace change.

In my businesses, I have the opportunity to teach, which I get so much happiness and reward from doing. Teaching is so rewarding.

As I continue to grow and prepare for tomorrow, I am so grateful and humble that I made this decision which changed my life, giving me an opportunity to live a life.

May your tomorrows be filled with love, good health, and prosperity.

To contact Jorge:

DIRECT: 561-320-1983

EMAIL: jorge@thebridgecoach.life

Website: www.thebridgecoach.life

Facebook: The Bridge – Life Coaching, LLC

Twitter: @thebridgecoach1

Skype: sober94

Sally K. O'Brien

With a master's degree in speech, administrative experience, and teaching English, speech, and writing for over twenty-five years in high school, community college, and university, Sally K. O'Brien is an Amazon best-selling author, professional speaker, trainer, life coach, certified confidence coach, and NLP Master Practitioner. Owner of her business, S.K. O'Brien/ Healing Hands Publishing, for twenty-eight years, she offers teleseminars, webinars, VIP Days, live interactive workshops and seminars, and weekend retreats on the Big Island of Hawaii for memoir writing and life coaching.

She was a contributing writer in *Creative Communicators* (1990); contributing writer in *Chicken Soup for the Soul at Work* (1996); Amazon best-selling author of *Love Offerings to the Universe* (2004); and contributing writer in *101 Great Ways To Improve Your Life, Vol. 2* (2006). O'Brien lovingly helps, guides, directs, and teaches her clients to write their own life stories. This former educator's passion is to work with those who want to share their life lessons, to know that their lives made a difference, and who want to leave their families a legacy.

Love You More: My Last Month with Lael

By Sally K. O'Brien

I remember my daughter Lael and I had an ongoing appointment to connect with each other every Sunday after I moved back to my spiritual home in Hawaii. On February 24, 2013, Lael said as we began our weekly conversation, "I am glad I chose you as my mother. I get my strength from you." I said, "Thank you. I am honored to be your mother." She paused and told me she had seen her oncologist on Tuesday, and found out she was on the cancer journey again after being cancer free for three years. I had discovered she had been diagnosed with breast cancer the week after Mother's Day in 2010.

Again, I was the first to be told before her older sister Lyra. However, her little sons were told on Saturday. Her oldest son was concerned about her losing her hair a second time. They also wanted her to leave it brown when it grew back and not go blonde again.

She and her husband of almost thirteen years had done a lot of research, and she was going for a second opinion to M.D. Anderson Cancer Center in Houston, Texas, which is the top cancer center in the United States. She had been diagnosed with bone cancer, and it was treatable. She was going to start radiation as she had done three years ago and also chemo as she had done before. The oncologist was optimistic.

Lael told me she had gotten out her Reiki manual and book and also Louise Hay's book, *Heal Your Body A-Z: The Mental Causes for Physical Illness*. She said, "I took care of the physical part before, and now I know I need to look at the mental. I've seemed to have not been successful or gotten it the first time, and this time I'm going to nail it!"

I said, "Lael, I've been doing Reiki distant healing for you since you were first diagnosed three years ago, and I will do it daily for you until I die." She said, "I know mother."

During our conversation, she was upbeat and determined. I asked her if she wanted me to fly in. And she said, "No." Later in the day, I emailed Herb, her husband, and asked to come back so he could accompany her to Texas around March 15, which was her scheduled appointment. I wanted him to be with her when she had her consultation. I would take care of my three little grandsons, ages four, six, and eight.

His email response back to me was, "No. Lael did not even want her sister Lyra to go with her. She has decided she wants to be by herself and not be concerned about meeting the needs of anyone else." I understood.

The following Sunday, I didn't speak with Lael. I knew she was traveling back and forth with radiation treatments. My inner guidance told me to wait for her to call me. On Sunday, March 10, I spoke very briefly to my daughter. On Monday, we talked again.

She told me she was losing weight and had bruises below her left eye and on her left leg. I had mentioned to Lael that I read the following from Ingrid Lorch Bacci's book *Effortless Pain Relief: A Guide to Self-Healing from Chronic Pain*: "The left side of the body represents the Feminine Principle, while the right side represents the

The Change

masculine. Your issues are connected to the women in your life." Her response was "Then you fix it!"

I learned during our conversation that she was now a patient at the Cancer Treatment Centers of America® in Zion, Illinois. They had done blood tests and found out she also had brain tumors. She was now doing cranial radiation, and she was not allowed to drive anymore because she could have a stroke.

On Tuesday, March 19, I found out the following from Herb in a Facebook post: *Challenging news about Lael's condition. Lael's liver was in distress. A CT scan revealed no cancer in the liver, but additional tests allowed the doctors to make a diagnosis of DIC (Disseminated Intravascular Coagulation) for which there is no treatment regimen.*

I wasn't told Lael was admitted to the ICU at the Cancer Treatment Centers of America® on Monday, March 24. I listened to a voice mail from Herb saying Lyra had taken the week off, and it was time for me to come in. He was not going to leave her side. When I returned his call, he stepped out of Lael's ICU room to speak with me.

"I am so proud of you."

"We're a team. I'm not going to leave her side."

I then got an opportunity to speak to Lael on the phone. "I'm coming in. Stay strong. I love you more."

I began preparations to fly back to Wisconsin. I had agreed to not show any emotion in my voice and no tears when I was around my daughter. I asked God to help me honor Herb's request. I flew out on Thursday and arrived in Milwaukee on Good Friday around 3:30 p.m. Steve met me at the airport. My daughter Lyra was at their Milwaukee home with Lael and Herb's sons instead of in Williams

Bay, their home. On the drive from the airport, Steve said, "Lael's liver is failing, and the DIC cancers are draining her."

When we arrived at my older daughter's home, Lyra and Steve's sons gave me hugs, and Lael and Herb's younger sons came to greet me when I stepped in the door. They hugged me and welcomed me. Their oldest son did not come down. I went upstairs to find him, and he shared with me what he was feeling and I listened quietly. After dinner, Lyra and Steve went out to purchase candy, eggs, and baskets. Easter was to be a distraction from what was going on with their mother in the hospital.

I will forever be grateful to Gail, Steve's mother from Illinois, who chose to drive several hours round-trip on Saturday to babysit Lyra and Steve's two little boys, ages 5 and 7, and Lael and Herb's three, so I could accompany them to see my daughter for the first time on Saturday. She was so kind and caring to me.

As I walked in Lael's ICU hospital room, she was sitting up in her bed wearing a yellow gown and she gave me a big smile. She told me I looked beautiful, and I realize now I discounted her compliment by saying, "I have no makeup on," instead of saying "Thank you." I handed her the framed picture of her family I had taken a year before in April 2012 at Lyra and Steve's older son's birthday party. She was visibly pleased with the picture and asked her husband to put it up on the window shelf. Then I handed her back the card we traded back and forth from 1999, when my daughters first sent me the mother lion and her three cubs card. She nodded, smiled, and said, "my little tigers" and received it back warmly.

Both my daughters mailed the card to me following my car accident on July 27, 1999. Enclosed was a check from them for $3,000 to buy a car to replace my totaled red convertible. I tore up the check and treasured the card, because it symbolized their love for me. When

The Change[8]

Lael was diagnosed with breast cancer in 2010, I sent it back to her in a care package of 40 little gifts because she was 40 years of age. And during my visit to their new home in Williams Bay, Wisconsin, in May 2012 shortly before I moved back to Hawaii permanently, she presented me with the card again. "It will be a loving reminder of your grandsons." We hugged, and I was so pleased by her generous gesture. I had glanced faithfully at the card on my coffee table in the living room every day I sat down on my sofa.

This second gift, too, went up on the shelf, so she could gaze at them from her bed. Those were the only objects I ever saw on her hospital window shelf. I observed her many affectionate glances over at them during the three times I got to be in her presence.

During our first four-hour visit, I asked to see Herb privately outside. I told him about the *Daily Word* monthly booklet I had given his oldest son upstairs, and the framed prayer from Unity which he had asked me to carry in my laptop case, so it wouldn't get broken. Herb told me he believed in God and gave his permission to let the boys display it in their bedroom.

I had also brought with me and presented to Herb the angel pin and told him the significance of it. I had purchased several angel pins and a statue at Angel Kisses religious gift shop in St. Charles, Illinois, in 1998 after I returned from doing the Journey of the Black Madonna Tour to France with a special girlfriend, Kate. My intention was to ask for a cure to my blindness in my right eye, not a healing. Before I left Lael and Herb's home in Chicago to fly back to Hawaii, I had gone to this store because I had read the feature article about Catholic rosaries turning into gold. Miracles had happened there.

On Easter Sunday, March 31, both families had lunch and watched movies with Lael. Even though she was tempted to drift off because of the medication, she remained alert and present for her sons and let them sit on her bed and touched them and welcomed their tender touching. That day, I was the last to leave her hospital room. I told her how courageous she was during our visit, and she nodded and seemed pleased with my acknowledgement.

Our last visit for our families with Lael began at 5 p.m. on Tuesday, April 2. As we all ate, we watched *Despicable Me 2* and laughed and shared happy memories. I told her during our visit, "You are an awesome mother!" She said, "Yes, I am!" Then I said, "And you have had an awesome career." That comment brought no reaction from my beloved daughter. I did not know that this would be the last time I would see her.

Once again, I was the last to leave her ICU room. As I watched Lyra embrace her before she left the room, I asked Lael if I could kiss her. She said, "Mother, you don't have to ask." I said, "Yes, I do." Then I kissed her forehead. As I turned back to her as I left her room, I said, "Love you more." She smiled at me one last time and nodded.

During the week, I watched my grandsons so Herb could be faithfully by his wife's side each moment. In hindsight, the outpouring of love and support from the people in this small community was phenomenal. They had lived in Williams Bay less than a year. At least one of Lael and Herb's friends showed up each weekday night to distract and create fun experiences and good memories for my grandsons. Several Williams Bay residents knocked on Herb and Lael's door with offerings of cooked meals or fruit baskets.

I also appreciated finding Lael's affirmation on an index card inside the Louise Hay book on their bedroom dresser. It read: "I am willing to release the pattern in me that is creating this condition." And I was grateful to discover she had recently borrowed from the Williams Bay Library Anita Moorjani's book, *Dying To Be Me: My Journey From Cancer, To Near Death, To True Healing*.

The Change[8]

During that continuing roller coaster week, first on Monday, the team of doctors told her to go home to die. They could do nothing more for her medically. She refused. When she woke up on Wednesday morning, she told her husband, "It is my destiny to die. I want to go home." Then a half hour later, the team walked in and told them both her numbers had changed, and there was a strong chemo which had a less than five percent chance of giving her another opportunity to live. My courageous daughter went for it! At first she had no side effects.

On Friday morning, Herb left the following voice mail: "Sally, it's Herb. It's a quarter to 7. We had a pretty good night. She slept well. Well, just calling you to remind you for 7 o'clock wake up for the boys. Also, I stopped on the way back to the hospital yesterday at the bakery in Lake Geneva and got a couple dozen of éclairs for the nurses. And Lael woke up this morning and the first thing she said was, 'I want an éclair.' And they had saved some for her. So she is doing okay. Things are good.

And I think Lyra is coming to the hospital today. Maxine and her boys are coming over for movie night tonight so that should be good for the boys. They should have a nice evening. . .Call me on the cell if you want. You should have a pretty easy day. Thank you for everything. We love you a ton! Bye."

In fact, Friday night, Herb called me and said, "Would you like to visit Lael on Saturday?" Then Saturday dawned and the ride was over. Her organs began to shut down, and she transitioned peacefully at 9:25 p.m. on Sunday evening, April 7.

On Monday, April 8, after Herb returned at 1 a.m., he woke his two oldest sons and told them their mother had died. He let the youngest of his sons sleep. When I came down in the morning, he had movies playing beginning with Lael's preparations for their first son's birth, and then progressing to Lael's pregnancy with all three of her boys.

Soon the house was filled with people. Lyra and Steve and my two grandsons arrived. There would be no funeral. Lael had donated her body to science.

I remember sitting across from Lyra and Steve and next to Herb. He reached over and took the angel pin out of his pocket, and said, "I want you to have this. Lael wore it on her necklace until she died." I remember he turned tenderly to me and said, "You can stay as long as you want."

At that moment, I knew he was back in charge of his sons and would be there for them to love and care for them and comfort them daily as they grieved together the loss of her physical presence. By the time I went to bed that night, my inner guidance had given me the knowing it was time to go back home to Hawaii for my own well-being. My body was telling me I needed to cry, grieve her loss, and heal surrounded by my friends, nature, and seeing and hearing the ocean.

After my return back to Hawaii, I received many condolence cards from friends, and yet, one stands out from all the others. I hope you will also find hope and comfort in its message, because during our lives, we will all grieve the loss of a beloved and cherished female. The verse begins on the card cover as you look at the single glittering pink rose with a glaze on top to hold a gold star in place and a second star at the top on the inside cover as you finish reading. "You'll feel her in the little moments, the stories, the familiar spaces she stepped in and out of. She'll be in your heart, forever a part of you, as sure as stars come out at night, as sure as love."

To Contact Sally:

Email: sobrien27@hawaii.rr.com, www.sallykobrien.com,

The Change[8]

(808) 238-5351, or mobile (414) 477-8987. In addition, for social media, Facebook and LinkedIn.

Kevin Audley

Kevin Audley MS.Ed., LPC fell two and a half stories off a roof in college over 30 years ago. After landing on cement and spending a week in intensive care with severe head injuries, Kevin went back to school with a new appreciation for life and his place in it.

Kevin has been a Licensed Professional Counselor and Coach for 19 years. He does not approach his clients in a traditional fashion and utilizes a revolutionary approach (Psych-K) to help his clients quickly reprogram their subconscious mind in two to three sessions.

He is the CEO of www.coachondemand.com – a global directory for Life and Business Coaches. He has written an internationally published book *What If You Were Your Own Best Friend?*

More recently, he is crowdfunding a movement to change the norm in the United States and Canada that it is appropriate to spank children as a form of discipline – www.nohitzone.com.

What If YOU Were Your Own Best Friend?

By Kevin Audley

What if YOU

Were your own best friend?

Hard to imagine

For most people

Never really considered

The best friend is out there

Somewhere

Right?

But what if…

You possessed the qualities

Of a best friend?

What kind of friend would you be?

Always supportive

Never judgmental

No conditions

A best friend would like you for you

Not for what you look like

Not for what you own

Not for what you can give them

Just show up

And they are there for you

Question is…

Why aren't you

Your own best friend

What could you do

How far could you go

How happy could you be

With you on your side?

Let me show you

Most of us "lead lives of quiet desperation." - Henry David Thoreau

Imagine for a moment what it would be like to have a friend who only loved you because you: were rich; had power; had status; were attractive; had a successful career; had an expensive car; had a Rolex watch; had a perfect body; had a lot of friends; had an advanced education; had a high IQ or certain athletic ability; had peachy white skin; were of a certain sex or ethnic background; had an attractive

The Change[8]

spouse; etc. Sound like a friend you would like to have? Most people would balk at the idea of associating with someone with such conditional regard for them. The fact is that we live with this person every day of the week. One look in the mirror will provide the identification. It is you—you do it to yourself. Most of us are never fully okay, happy, and accepting of ourselves. We hold out conditions that we must reach before we get there. We say we will arrive at this mythical state when the right person, job, or right situation comes along to complete our picture of what we think it is that we need. We delay it for the future when something outside of us occurs. Why did we change and why can't we just "be" happy without the checklist?

All of us need to believe they we are loved and lovable. When we began life, each was a given without question largely because we had no ability or desire to assess the situation. In the process of being socialized, we began to love ourselves and our place in the world based on condition. We became our own worst enemy.

Our socialization process has led us to believe that happiness is out there somewhere and always in the future. This goal-oriented and conditional approach to life is now the norm.

How is your life? Are you fully satisfied right now, or are you looking for something that might make it better? If you are like the majority of us, the grass is always greener somewhere else or down the line.

You were born perfect – in the process of life, you have forgotten your true nature.

I'm going to show you how to be your best friend once again – so stick with me here.

But first, in order to get to the payoff, I'm going to explain the many reasons why you haven't yet been able to be your best friend. You'll be amazed at what you—and everyone else—have been up against. I do this both to better help you understand your path (and have a better grasp of a societal system that's totally stacked against us), and because the more you understand something, the more its power to control you disappears.

The socialization process is necessary in a social world. The question is whether you want to step out of your illusions or live within them. You can be your own best friend. Because the first step is awareness, let's take a look at what you bought into as you learned to live in society.

The illusion of less than

The belief that we must go outside ourselves to get our needs met is a result of our initial separation from our mother. Imagine what it must have been like to be a young human in the mother's womb. Everything in the way of basic needs is provided. Plenty of food is being pumped in without even asking. No need to worry or go anywhere. All the child has to do is develop and "be" in the world. No external identity from that of the mother. Essentially, the fetus and mother are one, because in the child's perception there is no concept of separation. Hang out in the warm, uterine sea that mom provides and that is the extent of life as the fetus experiences it.

From the moment of birth, the infant quickly realizes at some level that the party is over. Psychologists often refer to the birthing process as a traumatic event. The amniotic fluid that once served as a warm sea is suddenly gone. Next, the fetus is turned upside down and squeezed through a very small opening. Finally, the cord is cut and separation as a concept has begun.

The Change[8]

The once connected child with no external demands is now separate and seemingly on its own. Survival is out of its control and totally dependent on the mercy of the outside world. Nothing is automatic and nothing is a given anymore. The external world is the source of one's initial ability to survive. Out of necessity, one must look outside oneself to meet one's needs. In addition to being separate, the child makes an initial conclusion of being "less than" others upon which its survival depends.

One of the earliest writers on this inferiority feeling was Alfred Adler, a disciple of Freud. According to Adler:

"We must assume that at the beginning of every psychological life there is a more or less deep inferiority feeling. Because he is exposed to the environment of adults, each child is tempted to regard himself as small and weak and to appraise himself as inadequate and inferior." (1912)

Adler sums it up by saying: "We all start out in life with a 'minus rating' and try to transform it to a 'plus rating.'"

The illusion of "less than" has a lot of support from others. The first unlikely proponents of this false conclusion were our parents.

Parents

First of all, there isn't a required parenting 101 class on how to raise a child. Most parents teach us what they learned in their family and what society dictates as normal. Their intentions were likely positive – to teach and protect us. Unfortunately, the qualities exhibited as children often came into conflict with our parents' goal of keeping us safe and teaching us what they believed we had to learn about life. In the process of being molded into the acceptable, "normal" picture they had for us, we had to give up some or all of our natural childlike characteristics.

Our parents' focus was generally based on what they could see – our behavior and emotions. Anything deemed inappropriate in our parents' eyes was quickly discouraged and likely replaced with a "more suitable" behavior. We do things right and they gave us praise. We do things wrong, and we were either scolded or praise was withheld. As a result of these differential reactions – children come to respond to their own behavior in self-approving or self-critical ways depending on how it compares with the evaluative standards of others.

According to Albert Bandura's Social Learning Theory, "people learn to evaluate their own behavior on the basis of how others react to it." (1972)

The problem with molding a child to fit a parents' standard is that kids have a tendency to generalize. Too much focus on behaviors kids exhibit may lead the child to believe they are flawed as a person. Parents often don't separate the behavior from the child. So, if you tell a child "he is bad" in regard to something he is doing enough times, he eventually may generalize to the belief that he is "bad" in general. The child comes to believe that they are what they do. "You made a mistake" becomes "I am a mistake" to a child.

In an attempt to be "good" and conform to Mom and Dad's wishes, they give up part of their true self to get approval. Kids then take this conditional approach to themselves out into the world. "I am only ok if I do certain things and get the approval of others." Unfortunately, the external rewards and approval aren't enough because the child still believes the mistaken generalization of being bad on the inside. That invalid conclusion was based on the first and most significant relationship of all – parent/child. Please also see the impact of spanking on kids – www.nohitzone.com

The Change[8]

School

The illusion of "less than" is a process that starts at birth and increases as our socialization progresses. The belief system that says one is "less than" is a mistaken conclusion made by a child. Nevertheless, the process of being socialized in our society supports this conclusion. The school system not only supports the notion of the subjective inferiority of a person, but throws in an objective measure (grades) into the mix as well.

Teachers, much like our parents, have an ideal picture of what is appropriate in the classroom. In order to enforce the "normal" etiquette, teachers import principles and techniques used to train the family dog—catch him doing something you want it to do and reward him. Any deviant behavior is met with punishment or lack of reinforcement. It is a theory of motivation, which essentially says – "do this and you'll get that." The approach is conditional and terribly authoritarian. Kids are rewarded for what they do well externally, rather than who they are as people.

Slowly but surely, the kids catch on to the requirements. To get approval from the person running the show, one must act a certain way. Doing so also allows one to avoid punishment. The school system is another reflection of our socialization process that leads one to mistakenly conclude that control over one's life is outside of us. Based on being corrected over and over by parents and teachers, kids may generalize to the belief that they are bad as a whole. Children give up their own views on life and conform to others' expectations of what they are supposed to be—more reinforcement for one's subjective feeling of being "less than" others.

In addition to all those corrections of their "bad" behavior, kids have to endure an objective measure of one's worth in the form of grades. Make good grades and you are considered a "good" student. Get bad grades and you are a "bad" student. Kids that don't perform well may be labeled "slow learners" or be put into a remedial class away from the group. Kids that do well may get a false sense of esteem by being put into an advanced placement with respect to his/her peers. Everything is based on some external measure. Kids are compared with one another or some average that exists in the minds of the professionals. Before entering school, feelings about one self were subjective. Maybe a person could dismiss all the negativity of others. But now, now we have a number—numbers are hard to argue with.

**Writer's pause—for brevity's sake, I had to shorten this section to meet the requirements of the book—please click below for a more detailed explanation of our social conditioning and solutions in my book: <u>*What If You Were Your Own Best Friend?*</u>

Religion

Another institution that sets out a conditional checklist of good and bad behavior is organized religion. We learn very early that God will punish us and send us to Hell unless we act in accordance with God's laws. The leaders of the church have twisted the teachings of great religious leaders and attempted to teach conformity by using fear of retribution as a weapon. Thus, people behave morally not because they believe it is appropriate, but because God wants them to behave that way.

Peers

The peer relationship should be different. *Webster's Dictionary* defines a peer: as a relationship of equal standing. In spite of the definition, the child has no experience of being in an equal situation with someone. Children go into this relationship of equality with the idea of being less than others. They take the view of themselves formed so far in life and approach every subsequent interaction in the same way. "I must be liked and approved by others. If not, I am a bad person." One's worth is dependent on some outside approval rating.

What are the ramifications of approaching life in such a manner? Thomas Harris wrote a book back in 1969 called *I'm Ok, You're Ok* that addresses the outcome. Basically, Harris explained a theory that we take four possible life positions in our approach to

Interacting with others:

I'm not ok – you're ok.

I'm ok – you're not ok.

I'm not ok – you're not ok.

I'm ok – you're ok.

Early interaction with others leads a child to the belief that they are not ok, and everyone else is ok (life position number 1). They enter into relationships with peers of equal status with the fear of not being liked. No one wants to be on the outside looking in when it comes to belonging to the "in group." So, kids do whatever they have to do to be accepted by their peers.

Romantic Relationships

The path to romantic love can be a very anxiety-provoking quest for a lot of people. Based on the past, people believe they have to earn another's love. To take this approach going into a relationship is similar to Harris' "I'm not ok, you're ok" life position. It is based on fear and the belief that happiness is dependent on receiving external love from another. Essentially, the person believes they will be ok if another approves of and loves them.

Work

Have you ever met someone at a party and the first question out of their mouth is: What do you do for a living? They want to know because they believe one's career says a lot about a person. The reality is that work is something we do – not who we are. In spite of this fact, society has a different take on the world of work. Individuals are judged as if their line of work is their identity, and their value as a person is rated accordingly. Using this logic, the individual defines one's worth based on this external factor. Some jobs are perceived to be better than the rest because of the status, power, and money that go along with them.

Advertising

Advertisers know something about us. We believe we have weaknesses. They pitch the product not only to reinforce the mistaken belief, but also claim to have the solution that will heal the wound we think we have. If you buy this, you will feel good and have all the good things life has to offer. It doesn't work, because no amount of external ingredients can lead one to achieve internal satisfaction. Once you add these products to your inventory, you will feel good for a while. The bad news is that the effects will wear off and you will need something else. Advertising is another example of the "training" by our society that reinforces the belief that we are not enough as we are in the present moment.

Albert Einstein once said "the tragedy of life is what dies inside man while he lives."

How to be your own best friend

The socialization process is necessary. There is no way to prevent the illusions that result. Now for the good news—the illusions are created by our thinking—which can be changed.

We have been living in fear—based on the idea of scarcity. We believe we are not enough. The solution according to what we are taught: "If I have or do enough, I will be enough."

How do you become ok as you are right now—without adding or doing anything? The answer lies in the deep dark recesses of your subconscious mind.

Many of the mistaken conclusions about our self are firmly in place by age five. William Wordsworth once said: "The child is the father of the man." He is right in that our beliefs about the world carry forward into our adult life.

These conclusions are hidden away from our awareness in the subconscious mind. This part of our mind comprises 90% of your belief system and is the storehouse for your habits and L/T memory. You cannot change your subconscious beliefs by thinking differently at a conscious level.

> "You can't think you way out of a problem at the level of mind in which it is created."~ Albert Einstein

So how do you go to a deeper level and actually make lasting change?

Unlike traditional talk therapy, I don't teach my clients to think differently by monitoring their negative self-talk and behaviors.

I work with them using a cutting edge technique called Psych-K. Utilizing this breakthrough technique, I actually help my clients reprogram their mind at a subconscious level. This wickedly effective technique can take as little as two to three sessions. How does it work?

Your life is a reflection of your beliefs. This statement is based on the science of quantum physics, as well as spiritual and metaphysical precepts. These beliefs—usually subconscious—are the cumulative effect of lifelong programming. As a result, we sometimes think and behave in self-defeating ways because the subconscious mind acts as a saboteur to the conscious mind.

PSYCH-K™ processes provide a user-friendly way to reprogram your subconscious mind by changing the beliefs that sabotage you into beliefs that support you...quickly and easily.

You will find Psych-K mentioned as a solution in the best-selling book by Bruce Lipton called *The Biology of Belief*.

To contact Kevin:

Kevin Audley 913-850-3639

info@coachondemand.com

Adrienne Slaughter

Adrienne Slaughter has been inspiring and motivating audiences since she was a teenager. When faced with two near-death experiences before the age of eighteen, she chose to share her stories "with a smile," attesting how a positive attitude allowed her to survive both. While traveling the nation as a keynote speaker at a young age, Ms. Slaughter was awarded Speaker of the Year from the United Way and Volunteer of the Year from the American Cancer Society. Then, facing another life-threatening hurdle in 2009, Ms. Slaughter recovered fully, with that positive attitude. Today, residing in Hermosa Beach, California, she enjoys every day to its fullest and continues to enthuse audiences nationwide. Her website www.AdrienneSpeaking.com highlights the many ways she is extraordinary and referred to as a "motivating dynamo." Her chapter "How an A-plus Attitude Turns Adversity into Achievement," will inspire YOU!

How an A-plus Attitude Turns Adversity into Achievement

By Adrienne Slaughter

As an athletic, community-active single woman living in Hermosa Beach, California, I live a wonderful life full of smiles. As a professional speaker, I inspire and motivate audiences of all types and sizes–from keynoting small fundraisers to emceeing large events. I also enjoy traveling nationwide and speaking to corporate leaders and their employees. Life is almost perfect. But it hasn't always been so easy. I faced my first of three major hurdles when I was just fourteen years old, and I was given only a one percent chance of survival.

The youngest of five daughters, I was raised to appreciate everything and to earn every dollar of my allowance. It wasn't much, but at least it was something. I say this because I was brought up in a very affluent neighborhood in Atlanta, Georgia–Buckhead. We belonged to Cherokee Town & Country Club, and I went to a private school—Lovett. My mother was a housewife, and my father was a corporate lawyer, after being raised in a lower class household. He respectably became a self-made man after fighting in World War II and the Korean War. I grew up in a mid-sized home on five acres. With that came yard work–raking the long driveway, picking weeds, and mowing the three lawns. My parents would stress that we must push hard and sometimes sweat to achieve our goals in life. "Earn it, Adrienne," they would say. Looking back, I am so glad they did.

In seventh grade, it was becoming apparent that I would not just be the "ball girl" on the tennis court while my parents and sisters played. I began to play myself, and very well, I might add. My father and I began to really "bond" on the tennis court. And he was good–very good. When he served, I would do my best just to return the ball over the net. But most of the time, he hit it so hard that I had to avoid being pummeled by his tennis ball!

Spring of eighth grade arrived and I was hitting better than any girl my age both at school and at the club. I won the spring backboard tournament and even started beating my father on the court. Cherokee's tennis pro/coach George Amaya saw my potential and suggested that I play tournaments. So I did–and boy, did I! That summer before ninth grade, I played all three Georgia state tournaments and either won or was runner-up in seven of the weekend matches. So, come fall, I received my first state ranking. All eyes were on me now, and photographers were shooting me.

Now came the real test–spring of ninth grade and spring tennis. It was a given that I would be playing #1 Singles and #1 Doubles for our Junior Varsity team at Lovett. But I was predicted and determined to move up to Varsity–as a fourteen-year-old ninth grader.

In the first singles tennis match on Monday afternoon, I was hitting the ball quite well and easily won. Then, in the middle of the doubles match, my right knee began to hurt. Although my partner, Kathy, and I still won, it was uncanny that my knee hurt for no apparent reason. On Wednesday, I played in our second team match against a big rival, Westminster. This time, my knee began to hurt in the middle of the singles match and continued throughout the doubles match. Afterwards, it was throbbing.

On Thursday, my knee hurt to walk up and down stairs at school, and the pain was getting progressively worse. After school, my

The Change[8]

mother called Dr. Funk, the orthopedic surgeon for the Atlanta Falcons football team and a very close friend. While it normally would have been a thirty-day wait to see Dr. Funk with NFL spring training, he squeezed me in the next day–Friday. Dr. Funk examined my knee, took X-rays and then pointed to a lump, which I had not seen before. He then asked me to stay off my knee that weekend and return to see him on Monday. No way! I had tennis practice over the weekend and not only was I preparing to move up to Varsity at school, but I was also predicted to be top ten in the South that summer. But with Dr. Funk's insistence and reassurance, I eventually agreed to take it easy.

On Monday, my mother and I returned to see Dr. Funk, and I brought a duffle bag "just in case" I needed to spend the night. I underwent a bone scan while lying nervously, all alone, in a big room on a huge cold table. Above me were bright orange lights on a monitor indicating exactly where that lump on my knee was. Sure enough, I had to spend the night. Tuesday morning I was given anesthesia and doctors took a biopsy, removing bone cells from my right knee. I awoke in the recovery room with my knee throbbing five times more painfully than it had after what would turn out to be my last tennis match at Lovett.

My parents arrived soon and wheeled me up to the hospital room where I was taught how to walk on crutches. The pain in my knee was still excruciating, even after I was given major painkillers "for a kid." Before I knew it, I was spending another night in the hospital. Now it was Wednesday, and the day crept by slowly. I began to miss my friends and especially my boyfriend. I wanted to be at school, in class, and on the tennis court, like normal. Instead, I was still in the hospital, on crutches, with no idea when this nightmare would end. Something was really wrong.

My parents were called in for a meeting with Dr. Funk while I remained alone in my room. I will never forget walking on crutches to the end of the hallway and seeing the bright sunset in the distance. I started to cry and say a prayer. I asked that I be able to return to the tennis court soon. You see, that was my number one priority.

My parents returned from their meeting. My mother walked in first with my teary-eyed father close behind. I had never seen my father with tears in his eyes–not ever. Mom sat at my bedside and said, "Adrienne, it's a tumor." At fourteen, I knew that that was bad, very bad. But I did not think of life or death because she did not use the "cancer" word–even though that was what it was. My first thought entailed not knowing my immediate future; I was scared. Within twenty minutes, Devereux, one of my best friends, arrived and then my boyfriend Lee. I was still crying, so my parents shared the news with them. They were also in a state of shock.

That evening, my parents consulted with Dr. Funk to decide on the next step. Dr. Funk knew the head surgeon at what was then the best cancer clinic with the "best cure rate" for childhood bone cancer. The decision was clear. Thursday morning, my parents and I were in the car driving to Shands Hospital in Gainesville, Florida. That six-hour drive was one of the worst times of my life–because I did not know what was next. When would I be back on the tennis court?

We arrived and met with Dr. Springfield, the head surgeon, on Friday morning. In a small room, with seven resident doctors surrounding Dr. Springfield, I sat in a wheelchair facing him, with my parents behind me. The doctor very straightforwardly said, "Adrienne, you have Osteogenic Sarcoma, childhood bone cancer. If you have a choice of surgery, we suggest amputation." He then shared that my other choices may include a human or artificial knee transplant, or a new surgery in which they would place a rod from mid-thigh to mid-shin. After he finished, he asked if I had any questions. I immediately asked, "Will I play tennis again?" He replied, "No."

The Change[8]

Although I had been sitting there, calmly listening, I was now crying. Crying the largest tears there could possibly be. Next, I was being wheeled down the hallway, into the elevator, and back up to my hospital room. During that long ride, I made a firm decision. I was going to prove Dr. Springfield wrong. I was going to play tennis again. I was going to even enjoy being pummeled by Dad's serves on the tennis court! I was going to play tennis again.

Tests returned and showed that the tumor had not spread; so I had a choice of surgery. My parents and I met with our resident doctor, Dr. Bittar, to discuss my options. For several reasons, including the fact that amputation scared the heck out of all of us, we chose the newer surgery with the rod. Still, Dr. Bittar had to ask for our consent "if something happened" necessitating amputation. We signed the form, hoping that its likelihood would be slim.

The big day arrived. Exactly fourteen days since the first pain in my knee on the tennis court, I was in surgery. With the tumor localized two-and-a-half days before, I was hopeful that I would have a leg when I awakened. Unfortunately, Dr. Springfield discovered that my tumor spread six inches over the weekend. Six inches! Because of its spread, the doctors were forced to amputate my right leg above the knee.

The following night I endured phantom pains, as my nerves still thought there was a foot at the end of my right leg. No matter how many pills the nurses gave me, I still felt as if a hammer were hitting my foot, a 50-pound weight toppling over my toes, and sometimes even an electric shock sensation. This went on all night. It was unbearable. Thankfully, the phantom pains eventually stopped the following day, but I was exhausted.

Finally, a few positives occurred–big positives. Because I was in tiptop shape, I was able to start physical therapy just two days after the amputation. A nursing student, Noelle Fedora, who had experienced the same surgery five years before, walked in–without a limp. Her hair, after having had chemotherapy, was long and beautiful. My fifteenth birthday was the next Monday, April 13th, one week after surgery. Our church minister, his wife, and my parents' best friends arrived from Atlanta that morning. A few minutes later, my boyfriend Lee, close friend Todd, and sister Elaine walked in. I was presented with three birthday cakes, one of which was extra special. Three cute boys from a fraternity at the University of Florida entered my hospital room with a big cake, all lit up with candles, singing "Happy Birthday." Wow. As a young girl turning fifteen years old, this was all amazing. But the most remarkable aspect of this day was that both Lee and Todd, also in 9th grade, accepted me, face-to-face, without a leg.

After the guests left that afternoon, I was immediately taken downstairs to begin radiation therapy to my lungs. You see, my type of bone tumor metastasizes to the lungs if not removed before one little cancer cell gets into the bloodstream. I learned later that the doctors were sure that had happened. So it was imperative that I begin this therapy as soon as possible. Every day for the next two weeks, I received major radiation to both lungs. It really was not so bad, as I did not feel nauseous, and I did not experience any immediate repercussions. Note that I say "immediate."

After the two weeks, my mother and I returned to Atlanta. The very first day we were back, I asked my father to grab my tennis racket and meet me near the backboard on the turnaround. Standing on one leg, I put both crutches under my left arm, dropped the tennis ball with my right hand and hit it against the backboard. Accomplishment! I was already close to proving Dr. Springfield wrong. Maybe I was not playing on a tennis court yet, but I would be soon. After just a few minutes, my father was crying, and then I started crying. Then I commented that he was now the ball boy, not

The Change[8]

me! We both started laughing, while at the same time crying. Soon my mother walked outside and joined us with tears and laughter.

By the fall, my father and I were hitting tennis balls at least once a week. My hair was growing back after the chemotherapy. I was still getting straight A's and I was receiving positive attention by playing tennis on TV. I started volunteering for the American Cancer Society so much that I was awarded Volunteer of the Year from the American Cancer Society and Speaker of the Year from the United Way–both at just seventeen years old. So, high school life was perfect–until the last day of eleventh grade.

I was in a horrific automobile accident. While sitting in the back seat of a convertible VW Rabbit, I was thrown upwards and I hit the roll bar when the driver lost control. The car went down a hill, and one tree kept us from flipping over and going down a steeper hill into a creek. After my parents were notified, they arrived to see flashing lights everywhere. They had to park the car and walk past the barriers, as the street had been closed. They had to be wondering whether or not I was still alive. My parents got to the scene, saw the totaled Rabbit, and their youngest daughter being lifted gently from the back seat–unconscious.

I was rushed to the nearest emergency room where it was determined that I had a subdural hematoma. The neurosurgeon was paged and immediately removed the blood clot, but I remained in a coma for four days. While in a coma, I missed my sister Linda's wedding, which was celebrated with a reception in our own backyard. After being hospitalized for a month, the doctors allowed me to return home to join my sister Diane visiting from Dallas, as long as there was a private nurse in my bedroom. I had a long road ahead of me.

Then a very special thing happened. A letter came in the mail, reading that I had been accepted for a modeling job at Saks Fifth Avenue. So two months later, I began modeling–with a wig, my right arm in an above-elbow cast, and a prosthetic leg. How marvelous was that?!

After recovery, my eventful life continued. I still played tennis, graduated from high school and college, worked in the corporate world, and was flown around the nation to speak. I was enjoying life to its fullest, and I was even invited to ski in the Paralympics. Yes, on one leg, I say proudly. Then in 2009, I had my first mammogram. You guessed it–breast cancer.

Cancer. Again? Well, the next few weeks were extremely challenging, to say the least. I underwent more and more tests and then endured one of the worst experiences imaginable, a biopsy to my breast. Independent as I have always been, I drove myself to the clinic alone. That was a big mistake. I had to lie on a cold steel table in the most uncomfortable position, with my head turned upward and my neck feeling like it might crack. I had to be completely still; I could not move an inch. Then, because I moved just a little, the doctor had to do it all over again. When finished, I looked across the room and saw a large screen with fuzzy lights in three places. Was that my breast? Was the cancer in several spots? I broke down and started crying uncontrollably when the nurse's assistant rushed to turn the screen off. Ridiculous.

Soon though, there was a positive turning point. I learned several bits of good news, including that the cancer was in stage zero, the earliest stage. Neither chemo nor radiation therapy would be necessary. The breast cancer was not genetic. In fact, its source was the radiation therapy that I had received to my lungs/breast area, the very therapy that saved my life twenty-eight years before. Fortunately, I was so fit that I was able to take advantage of a fifteen hour DIEP flap surgery with breast augmentation.

Even though the cancer was only in my right breast, I chose to have a double mastectomy. It made sense to me because I had received

The Change[8]

radiation to both lungs and both breasts–so there was a huge chance that I would get cancer in my left breast. Well, I did. Even though the mammogram and MRI detected cancer only in my right breast, the pathologist discovered cancer in my left breast as well. Since I chose to have the double mastectomy, I was now 100% cancer-free, surviving again.

While my professional tennis-playing career never happened, I achieved much more–against the odds. You see, I had an incredible team of support around me–and faith. Yes, I had faith in God, but faith in one's self is so important. Faith in one's self is so needed to overcome obstacles in life. With my family and friends, and a positive attitude, I beat those odds and have been called a "miracle."

Today, I enjoy life to the fullest–again. I not only play tennis but also rock climb, ski, snorkel, and dance. Excuse my candor, but I really am more active than most two-legged men and women. I even danced in the Rio de Janeiro Carnival and recently tossed the First Pitch at Dodgers Stadium. There are special reasons for me to be here, still enjoying this phenomenal life. In addition to inspiring, motivating, and empowering individuals one-on-one and audiences, I also uplift as an author. My goal is to bring more smiles to the world, as I speak and write with a smile every day.

A positive "can-do" attitude is everything. With it, I survived that car accident. With it, I beat cancer twice–at fourteen years old, having only one percent chance of survival, and again in 2009. I won the best three set match–that is the match of life. You see, an A-plus attitude really does turn adversity into achievement!

To Contact Adrienne:

www.AdrienneSpeaking.com

Facebook.com/AdrienneSlaughter13

Twitter: @AdrienneSpeakin

www.youtube.com/channel/UCypVBMaOv7sDr7QfkbHdEjA

(310) 940-9200

Afterword

Life is always a series of transitions... people, places, and things that shape who we are as individuals. Often, you never know that the next catalyst for change is around the corner.

Jim Britt and Jim Lutes have spent decades influencing individuals to blossom into the best version of themselves.

Allow all you have read in this book to create introspection and redirection if required. It's your journey to craft.

The Change is a series. A global movement. Watch for future releases and add them to your collection. If you know of anyone who would like to be considered as a co-author for a future book, have them email our offices at support@jimbritt.com.

The individual and combined works of Jim Britt and Jim Lutes have filled seminar rooms to maximum capacity and created a worldwide demand.

The blessings go both ways, as Jim and Jim are always willing students of life. Out of demand for life-changing programs and events, Jim and Jim conduct seminars worldwide as well as created a global company in over 170 countries called Quanta International that allows anyone to benefit behaviorally as well as financially.

If you would like to hear more about how the Quanta Company can assist you in both income generating and personal development, please email our offices at: quanta@jimbritt.com.

To Schedule Jim Britt or Jim Lutes as your featured speaker at your next convention or special event, email: support@jimbritt.com

Master your moment, as they become hours that become days.

Your legacy awaits.

Blessings,

Jim Britt and Jim Lutes

www.ingramcontent.com/pod-product-compliance
Lightning Source LLC
Chambersburg PA
CBHW070534010526
44118CB00012B/1134